The
Champlain Canal:
Mules to Tugboats

Capt. Fred G. Godfrey

_____*LRA Inc.*_____
Monroe, New York
1994

_____*LRA Inc.*_____
Dunderberg Road, RD#6-Box 41
Monroe, New York 10950-3703

Library of Congress Cataloging-in-Publication Data

Godfrey, Fred G., 1915-
    The Champlain Canal: Mules to Tugboats by Fred G. Godfrey.
    122p.
    Includes photos, maps, index.
    ISBN:0-912526-66-1
    1. Champlain Canal (N.Y.) -- History 2. New York State Barge Canal System (N.Y.) -- History 3. New York (State) -- Social life and customs I. Title
HE396, C338G63   1994
366'.48'097473 -- dc20   94-8386
                                           CIP
                                           AC

This book owes its existence to
Craig Williams
who suggested, urged,
and pushed me to write it,
providing encouragement and much material.

Contents

Preface

The Old Champlain Canal
Photo, Fred Godfrey

As time slides along its inexorable path, we humans do not realize the history we may witness, and which we fail to record. The events of today are the history of tomorrow but we do not recognize it until much later.

Such could be said of the old Champlain Canal and the people who were involved in its construction, operation, maintenance, and use. It was completed from Fort Edward to Whitehall at the end of 1819, officially opened for its full length September 10, 1823, and was superseded by the Champlain Barge Canal in 1915. Less is known of the daily life of the canal boat families who made a living on this vibrant waterway and of the businesses that grew up along its shores.

Today the old canal is nearly forgotten. In some areas it is a weed-grown ditch containing stagnant water. Other areas are completely lost to view with houses built where the canal once was. The old wooden locks are gone as are the businesses along its banks. Stone-built locks survive such as Bassett's Lock alongside Route #4 south of Fort Miller. Lock #15, the Brewery Lock in Fort Edward, is almost completely buried under decomposing vegetation and the trash of the years.

It is fortunate that the Canal Society of New York State has audio tapes which tell about this old way of life during the last days of the canal. These tapes were made by Albert Gayer of Schenectady, New York and feature stories told by Captain Louis Vandervoort, who used his old log books for reference. Contributions were also made by Captain Frank Godfrey, Captain Daisy Godfrey, Captain Austin "Snub" Huftil, Captain Bob Leddick, Al Vandervoort, William Cleary, and Herb Beatty.

The credentials of these people follows:

Louis Vandervoort, of the family of pioneer tugboat men in the old Champlain Canal, spent his working years taking part in the changes that took place there over the years.

Frank Godfrey went on a canal boat as a boy, ran canal boats as a teenager, married, and ran canal boats for a short time before going on tug boats and becoming master and pilot, working most of the waters of northeastern United States including the Great Lakes and coastwise.

Daisy Godfrey, whose father, Dick Knight of Port Henry, N.Y. had operated schooners on Lake Champlain and boats on the canal, married Frank and merged her career with his while raising a son and a daughter. She held a master's and pilot's license of about the same area as her husband. During World War II, Frank was master of the *Eugenia Moran*, son Jack was First Mate, and wife Daisy was Second Mate. They operated off the Atlantic coast and were awarded the North Atlantic Medal.

Austin Huftil of Waterford, N.Y. was a third generation boatman who started as a driver at age seven and finished as a tugboat captain and pilot from Buffalo, N.Y. to New York City harbor. As did many other boating families, he had a daughter born on his canal boat at Pier 5, East River.

Captain Bob Leddick, of Schuylerville, grew up on canal boats and like many others made the transition to tugs. Early in my career I served a few days as deckhand under Bob when, late in his career, he was mate on a Lake Champlain Despatch Company tugboat.

Al Vandervoort, older brother of Louis, was engineer on many tugs throughout the period of this book.

William Cleary, whose grandfather of the same name was a major stockholder in the Lake Champlain Transportation Company (known as The Line), was a canal buff and collector of canal stories.

Herb Beatty of Glens Falls, who followed in his father's footsteps by becoming a canal boatman, had many adventures during a lifetime on the water.

Most of the material that follows is taken from those tapes. I am indebted to the Canal Society and its president, Thomas Grasso, for allowing me to use them. This book will not attempt to give a full history of the canal but will describe the waterway and relate stories of its operation in the early twentieth century. It was at this time that the little tugs appeared and competed for the towing then done by horses and mules. After a short twelve year period this competition ended when the Champlain Barge Canal opened and animals could no longer be used. With the bigger canal came bigger tugs and the little ones were soon gone. This book records some of the events of this period and also gives a brief look at the later history of the canal.

Lock chamber at St. Jean, P.Q., Canada.
Note 5 layers of cut stone set on wood below.
Photo, Frank Godfrey

Canal boats at St. Jean, P.Q., Canada.
Chambly Canal.
Photo, Canal Society of NYS

Chapter 1

Captain Daisy Godfrey

T he following speech was given by Capt. Daisy Godfrey to the Canal Society of New York State at the
Queensbury Hotel, April 23, 1960.

The old Champlain Canal from Waterford to Whitehall
was approximately sixty-four miles in length, with twenty-three
locks, a depth of five feet, and a bridge clearance of eleven feet
above the water.

The boats, which completely filled the locks, were ninety-
seven feet long, eighteen feet wide and loaded to a depth of four
feet two inches southbound, and four feet four inches northbound,
which was gradually increased until 1904 when four feet six
inches was the loading draft for either direction. At four feet six
inches in draft these boats, on an average, carried 150 to 165 gross
tons depending on the build of the boat. There were, however,
two boats, the *Gilbert R. Green* and the *Ned Baker*, built at
Champlain, N.Y. which for a short time carried 180 to 190 gross
tons. These boats were of very light construction. The bow frames
were only 3 inches by four inches and the sides 3 inches thick
fastened together with ½ inch drift iron. The bottoms of these
boats were built of 4 inch spruce planks, edge drift bolted, with
no sister keelson nor floors. The center of these bottoms were
jacked down giving them a nine inch crown which, with the light
construction, allowed the ends of the bottom planks to project just
above the surface of the water when the boats were light. Due to
the nine inch crown in the bottom, when loaded to canal draft of
4'6" they were drawing five foot three inches through the center
of the bottom and were really overloaded.

At Waterford and Whitehall all boats were gauged. Gauge collectors, who issued clearances, measured the boats at all four corners by means of a pole which had a right angle iron on the bottom end and reached about six inches under the edge of the boat. This measuring stick was marked with sharp headed tacks which showed the draft of the boat. As soon as the state realized why these boats were having trouble at the locks they issued new gauges or measuring sticks which reached nearly to the center of the bottom of the boat. The crown was then taken out of the bottom. Because of the frail construction, these boats only ran a few years and were then abandoned.

The boatmen of both the Champlain and Erie Canals called the Hudson River the North River, the Erie the western canal, and the Champlain the northern canal. The word barge was never applied to boats on the canal until after the new Barge Canal was completed.

The runs, or routes, of the northern boats were Ottawa, Three Rivers, Quebec, New York, Philadelphia, Baltimore, and all intermediate places. Northern boats, at times, could be found as far south as Georgia, north to Murray Bay, west to Buffalo, and on Long Island Sound.

There were numerous kinds of cargo. Among these were coal, moulding sand, pottery clay, kerosene, lumber, paper, paper pulp, baled shavings, iron ore, pig iron, ice and hay. In the fall, a great many loads of apples and potatoes were loaded at places on Lake Champlain and the canal as far south as Stillwater.

The years 1888-89 are remembered and spoken of by all of the older canal men as "the season of the ice." The winter of '88-89 was a very mild winter. There was very little snow and the Hudson River did not freeze. As refrigeration was unknown at that time, New York depended upon the Hudson River to supply their needs. Therefore, ice was cut in the bays and coves along Lake Champlain and the canal. Stacked on the boat, square cut, covered with hay, straw, or sawdust to keep it from melting, the ice was shipped to New York by canal boat the summer of that year.

Just above and to the westward of Glens Falls, on the Hudson River, is Big Bend. Here is the only place on its course to the sea that the Hudson River flows north. In the latter part of

751 – Le Port, Saint Jean P.Q. Canada. The Harbor. St.Jean P.Q. Canada.

Robert H. Cook, **unidentified tug, and canal boats
at St. Jean, P.Q., Canada heading south.
The large coaling station was not there when I made
my first remembered trip to St. Jean in 1932.**
Photo, Frank Godfrey

The *Protector* on Lake Champlain for The Line.
Photo, Fred Godfrey

3

Defender on Lake Champlain with Line tow.
Photo, Fred Godrey

Whitehall, N.Y., April 27, 1905
Photo, NYS Archives

the winter of 1888-89, thousands of tons of ice were cut and stacked on the shores of Big Bend. With the opening of the canal in the spring, and during the summer, Glens Falls boats were locked into the river, pulled upstream to Big Bend, and loaded with ice for New York. My father told me that during the hot weather the ice melted so rapidly in those small boats that they would leave Glens Falls with about 100 tons of ice and deliver about 15 to 20 tons at New York.

I do not remember the length of the Glens Falls boats. I think it was something like 85 or 86 feet. The width however, was 14 feet and the height of the sides was 6 to 7 feet.

The northern boats delivered good-sized cargoes. At one time, a number of northern boats had a steady run from Port Henry to Wilmington, Del. with iron ore. These boats were loaded to a draft of 7 feet at Port Henry, part of the cargo on deck, and the boats lightered at Whitehall to a canal draft of 4 feet 4 inches. Some of the Glens Falls boatmen, with their teams, made a steady business of lightering these boats at Whitehall, taking the lighter load to Troy where it was reloaded. The Glens Falls boats had no stables and the teams were stabled at night in barns along the canal.

Here is a transcript from one of our old logs of a trip from Calumet, which is on the Ottawa River about 15 miles below or east of the city of Ottawa, to New York City. At that time, the Barge Canal was in use from Whitehall to Fort Ann and the old canal from there to Waterford. There are two points of special interest to be found in the log notes. One is a note on a storm while on Lake Champlain. The other is the Cornell Steamboat *Oswego* which was the last of the side-wheel steamboats used in towing on the Hudson River.

June 15, 1914 The canal boats *Alonzo F. Burt* and *George C. Donahue* completed loading lumber at Calumet.

The boats waited for tow until 6:30AM, June 18, at which time they cleared in the tow of the Ottawa Transportation Company tug *Harris*.

From 8AM to 12:30PM they were being towed by teams through the Granville Canal. On the Ottawa River the tug, when arriving at one of the canals, took the first boat through the canal and the other boats towed by teams.

10PM, June 18 to 1PM, June 19 in the Carillon, or as it was called, the Carry All Canal.

8:30AM to 12 o'clock noon at St. Anne's Canal.

From 4:30 to 7:30PM lying at La Chine waiting for McNaughton canal tug.

7:30PM June 19 until 1AM June 20, La Chine to Montreal in the La Chine Canal.

1AM June 20 Cleared Montreal in tow of the McNaughton Towing Company side-wheel steamboat *Hudson* and arrived in Sorel 9AM June 20.

June 20, 1:20PM Cleared Sorel in tow of side-wheel steamer *Rival* with 38 boats in tow.

June 20, 7:30 PM Arrived St. Orrs lock.

June 21 Tow was locked through and cleared at 4AM. Arrived at Chambly 5PM.

June 22 Cleared Chambly 5AM and arrived at St. Jean, which is the end of the Chambly Canal, at 2:45PM. The tow stayed at St. Jean waiting for one of the Lake Champlain Transportation tugs.

June 23, 11PM Left in tow of the tug *Protector*.

June 24, 11AM to 4PM clearing customs at Rouses Point. June 24, 11PM Southeast of Point au Roche we encountered a very heavy electrical storm. Winds of gale force which changed directions so rapidly that there was very little sea but heavy rain and very heavy chain lightning. The entire tow of 38 boats and tug were struck by lightning. Lanterns and light poles on the *Burt* and the *Donahue* were destroyed but no other damage. Lights on the tug were also destroyed. All other boats in the tow had from moderate to very heavy damage.

6

Captain Robert Lester and his wife were in their cabin at the time the lightning struck the cabin's stovepipe, blew the stove apart, and exploded in the cabin. The captain and his wife were nearly strangled by the fumes from the lightning before they could escape to the deck. Several of the boats that were struck by lightning started leaking and the hand pumps were operated steadily until the tow reached White-hall.

June 26 Arrived Whitehall 4:30AM and departed 9AM.

June 30 Arrived Waterford 9AM and arrived Troy 7:30PM. The *Donahue* discharged its cargo of lumber in the old Erie Canal at the dock of L. Thompson & Co., Albany.

July 3, 6:30PM Cleared Albany in Cornell tow with the side-wheel steamer *Oswego*.

July 6, 4PM Arrived Pier 5 East River, New York City, *Burt* towed to Dodge & Bliss Co., West End, Jersey to discharge.

**One of the places a canal boat might
load coal for Canada.**
Photo, Frank Godfrey

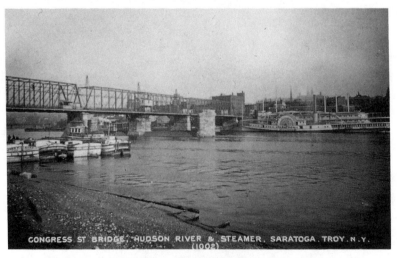

CONGRESS ST BRIDGE, HUDSON RIVER & STEAMER, SARATOGA, TROY, N.Y.
(1002)

**Congress St. Bridge: Hudson River and
Steamer, *Saratoga*. Troy, N.Y.**
Photo, Frank Godfrey

Chapter 2

Team Trip

What follows might be a typical trip for a Champlain Canal boat which loaded coal somewhere in the New York Harbor area or from a coal dock along the Hudson River such as at Cornwall, N.Y. for delivery in Canada. The boat would be placed in the Beverwyck tow out of New York for Albany. This might consist of forty to one hundred or more canal boats in a tow of a big tug with a small helper tug to pick up or land boats along the river. The Beverwyck tow was made up only of canal boats. The Cornell Steamboat Company of Rondout, N.Y. had other river tows of a mixture of barges, brick scows, ice boats, and other nondescript vessels. The ice boats were large vessels, pointed on each end, which carried ice to New York City before the time of electric refrigeration. The ice was harvested from the Hudson River in winter, stored in ice houses on shore until summer, and then loaded on the ice boats for shipment to New York. Despite being packed in sawdust or other insulating material, the ice melted somewhat. A large windmill on each boat operated a pump which kept the boat pumped out.

When the tow arrived at Albany, the little individually-owned tugs in the area would swarm around the tow like flies on a dung heap. Each captain on the little tugs would try to get the towing job from one or more of the canal boats. The tow would be picked apart right there in the river and there would be fewer boats to land at Albany. As the towing arrangements were completed, the tug would tow the boat to the sidecut at West Troy (Watervliet) if they were going up the Erie. Northbound boats could also go into the canal by way of this sidecut but preferred to go through Sloop Lock at Troy and enter the Champlain Canal via the Waterford Sidecut. The towing fee from Albany to Troy was four to six dollars, hard cash. This might be cut slightly if competition was very great or the boat was lightly loaded. The tug *Thomas Miller Jr.*, owned by George Cooley, was available to tow from Sloop Lock in Troy to Waterford for a fee of two dollars. At this point, a series of three locks raised the canal boat up into the Champlain Canal. Fred Bass had a team which towed vessels through theses three locks, up past Broad Street bridge to the Canal Collector's office to be gauged. This was a a brick building at a place that was built for a weighlock. Boats were not weighted but were gauged for depth, yet the building was still called The Weighlock.

Allowable depth from 1904 on was 4 ½ ft. On the Erie, it was deeper. The gauger used a stick with a piece of iron at right angles on the bottom to measure the depth of the boat. If deeper than 4 ½ ft., some cargo was supposed to be removed until the correct draft was reached. The boat owner could avoid this by making an unofficial cash adjustment with the gauger and be allowed to go on. It was said that some of the sticks were marked so as to show the boats loaded deeper than they actually were. If the canaler refused to make a cash settlement, then the boat had to be lightened to reach the acceptable draft. A sufficient amount of coal would be unloaded, perhaps five to ten tons. The gauger, as agent for the state, was responsible for this coal, but he would sell it to someone who would, in turn, retail it to people in the village. Everyone involved made money on the deal except the boat owner who lost time because of the unloading. The gauger did very well by pocketing the cash received from the sale. One gauger, when he retired, said he made fifty thousand dollars extra on that job. Captain Austin "Snub" Huftil said a couple of gaugers in Waterford became millionaires from working there. I feel sure this is a great exaggeration but undoubtedly the gaugers had a great source of extra income.Southbound boats gauged at White-hall. Glens Falls Feeder boats didn't gauge until they arrived at Waterford. It was rumored that they had an arrangement with the gauger for a standard fee regardless of their draft.

The coal was weighed on the boats when loading but was not weighed when discharged in Canada. Very few coal boats arrived at their destination with the same amount of coal that they

Sloop lock, Troy

Sloop Lock, Troy, N.Y. *Nellie* **of Glens Falls on right is
a Feeder canal boat, smaller than** *Katie Buell* **of
Burlington, Vt. a regular northern boat.**
Photo, Frank Godfrey

Waterford side cut.
Photo, Canal Society of NYS

Broad St., Waterford, N.Y.
Photo, Canal Society of NYS

Weighlock at Waterford, N.Y. looking north.
Photo, NYS Archives

This was the logo of the
Lake Champlain Transportation Co.
At one time it was painted on the bow of each tug
just aft of the name. It also appeared on some of the
galley dishes. I saw a few pieces years ago but have
been unable to locate any since then.

Line team and driver.
Photo, NYS Archives

13

Flynn's Lock
Photo, Canal Society of NYS

Hewitt's Lock, Mechanicville, N.Y.
Photo, NYS Archives

14

**North from Saratoga Ave.
Mechanicville, N.Y.**
Photo, NYS Archives

Champlain Canal at Stillwater.
Photo, NYS Archives

Sept. 26, 1906 Change bridge: allows team to cross to tow-path on other side of canal without unhitching tow line.
Photo, NYS Archives

Champlain Canal at Schuylerville.
Photo, NYS Archives

16

started with. The boater might use a little or drop off some to a friend along the way. Some locktenders such as Eddie Welch at the Lower Two Lock, had two woven baskets and a shovel used for taking their cut of the cargo. The boatmen seldom objected because it was no loss to them and it didn't hurt to have the goodwill of the locktender. Welch had a miniature coal yard which was maintained two baskets at a time.

Captain Frank Godfrey told a story about this custom of taking two baskets of coal. In his very early youth, Frank and his brother George (my father), were southbound with two light boats towed by a line team when they approached the lock but could not get the locktender out to open the gate and had to tie up the tow on the towpath. They could see the man standing in the window looking at them and smoking his pipe. Frank went down and had a heated altercation with the reluctant worker and finally got locked down and on his way again. They went to New York and loaded clay for St. Jean, P.Q., Canada. On the return trip they arrived at this lock on a very dark night. Hatches are kept on over the cargo hold when carrying clay but the first boat had a few hatches temporarily removed so a lock line could be tied around a midship cross beam. George took the boat into the lock and the locktender called to him, "What kind of coal you got on?"

"Red ash chestnut on this one." was the reply. "Stove coal on the other one. Take all you want."

The coal stealer threw his two baskets and shovel in and jumped in after them. When loaded with coal, the hold was almost full and a man could get back on deck from the coal pile. No so with clay. It is smaller in bulk than coal and slippery so the man could not get out of the hold. George shouted back to Frank on the second boat. "There is no locktender here. You'll have to do your own locking." George finished locking the first boat and Frank locked up the second one. They were coupled together and the mules started up the towpath. George went into his cabin and Frank was steering when he thought he heard voices. The Line Driver said he wasn't talking, not even to the mules. Frank said he could hear voices on the boat. His brother came out and told him about the reluctant passenger in the hold. A ladder was put down into the hold and an angry clay-smeared man came out with

17

his two baskets and shovel. The boats were swung in close to the towpath and the man jumped off. he had a walk of at least a mile carrying his equipment back to the lock. Frank did not say what the future relations were with this locktender.

A boatman on the Erie carried his own team aboard in a stable in the bow. The animals would be put ashore or brought back aboard by means of a horse bridge which was a sturdy gangway to reach from the boat to the towpath. The Champlain Canal boats did not have stables so the boat owner, after getting his clearance, left the Weighlock in tow of a line team or a trip team. The Line, as the Lake Champlain Transportation Company was called, was a large company with offices in Whitehall. They operated a fleet of tugboats on Lake Champlain, owned canal boats, leased canal boats, and provided mules for towing along the Champlain Canal. Barns were provided for these animals along the route at approximately twelve mile intervals. As you would guess, they were called Line barns. These mules towed three or four to a boat and were in single file. The driver would go from one barn to the next and then be replaced by another driver and team. If no relief was available they would rest six hours and then go on. There were Line barns at Waterford, Baker's Lock (between Mechanicville and Stillwater), Schuyler-ville, Fort Edward, Fort Ann, and Whitehall. There were also barns and resting places along the canal where a trip team could stop, feed, water, and rest. A team of animals would start work about three or four in the morning and stop about six thirty to feed except that when towing with the current, or with a light tow, the animals might have a feed bag hung on their heads to allow them to eat without stopping. At noon they might be stopped in a shady spot for a rest. The driver for The Line would go until he reached the next Line barn where the barn boss would give him his orders. Another muleskinner and team would be assigned to the boat and it would go on. The boat in tow of a Line team could go all day and all night if the teams were available.

Drivers of the trip teams would stop at whatever rest stop was convenient when the horses were tired. Some trippers used tow carts. These were small two-wheeled vehicles with a seat for the driver and were hitched behind the team and the towline

**Lock at Northumberland called
Lower River Lock.**
Photo, Jim Petit

Nov. 12, 1950 Lock #12, Bassett's Lock
Photo, Jim Petit

A Northern boat just fits into the lock.
Photo, NYS Archives

Basin at Fort Miller.
Photo, Jim Petit

Moses Kill at Patterson's Store looking north.
Photo, Jim Petit

**Boat once owned by my great-grandfather,
Henry Walrod, at Patterson's.**
Photo, Frank Godfrey

21

**This might be boatyard operated by
George Henry Sanders at Moses Kill.**
Photo, Jim Petit

Fort Edward looking south from Notre Dame St.
Photo, Canal Society of NYS

22

hitched to the back of the cart. Trip teams were usually two horses, rarely two mules, which unlike the Line teams, worked side by side. The name comes from the fact that they hired on for the complete trip, one way. Some were teamsters regularly engaged in this work while another might be a farmer with a team who had time to make a little extra money. The canal ran right through the farmlands so the boatmen and farmers were sometimes in contact and made deals for the towing. This farm team would hook onto a lumber boat at Whitehall and tow it to Waterford for twenty-five dollars. If it was an extra good pair of animals they might do it in three days. Towing northbound would cost more and take longer because it was against the current and northbound coal boats were deeper than southbound lumber boats.

One could tell when a Line tow was approaching because the mules were in line. If the team was two horses abreast one knew it was a trip team towing a Union boat or an independent. On the Erie animals could be used three abreast but the narrower towpath on the Champlain made it undesirable. Union boats were members of the Inland Seaman's Union. This organization was formed by the boat owners to provide opposition to the Line. They feared that The Line, with its equipment and facilities, would monopolize the freight on the canal and also be in a position to charge exorbitant towing fees. An office was maintained by the Union in Waterford and one in Whitehall. All their towing went to the trip teams.

To resume this fictitious trip — The boat in tow of a trip team left the Weighlock and was pulled along for two miles and came to the Lower Two Lock. Just past it was the Upper Two Lock. They received those names because they were close together and they replaced a series of three old wooden locks. Next came a three mile level to Flynn's Lock and a one mile level to Hewitt's Lock. Here George Reed operated a grocery store but later sold to to the Legetts. Both named were locktenders. The next four miles to Baker's Lock were hard towing. There were many places where the two boats could not meet without becoming wedged, with the consequence of more hard work and loss of time. There was no comparison between this and the Erie which was deeper, wider, had some locks side by side, and was better maintained. An old saying was that if you could boat on the Champlain Canal, you could boat anywhere. A number had been given to each lock in the canal but the boatmen of that day always referred to them by name. Next came the "long level," sixteen miles to Schuylerville.

After passing Stillwater, the boat went past the haunted house. Strange things had been seen on the towpath there are night and many boatmen were convinced that stretch was haunted. another place said to be haunted was the little yellow house on the towpath at Moses Kill. Pack peddlers operated along the canal and supposedly one had been murdered there and buried in the cellar. Bob Leddick, as a boy driving a team for his father, was convinced it was haunted and would try to hurry the team past it, much to his father's annoyance.

At Bemis Heights there was a high board fence along the towpath. This separated the canal from the Hudson Valley Railway tracks. Noise and lights from the trolleys scared the teams and the high fence helped to keep the animals calm. Up to this time, the towpath had been on the right side of the canal. Just before getting to Schuylerville Lock, the towpath was on the left or west side. The team got across to this new side by means of a change bridge. This structure had a ramp which the team walked up, crossed over the bridge to the other side, walked down a ramp which headed back the way they had come, and turned under the bridge and were on the changed towpath. The towline had been allowed to slide along the rail on the bridge and continued in use hooked to the team and the tow. These bridges were constructed so that the towline was always on the downstream side so the current in the canal would keep the line away from the bridge. This was the first changebridge since leaving Waterford.

At Schuylerville, the boat arrived at the River Lock which raised boats from the level of the canal up to the level of the Hudson River, called the North River by boatmen. In midsummer, when the river was very low and the water levels were almost equal, the lock gates might be "pressed" which meant left open at each end. This saved the time for locking but made for very hard towing going up against the current through the lock but very easy going down. After going through Schuylerville Lock, or the

Fort Edward - North from East St. bridge.
Photo, NYS Archives

Old Champlain Canal at Fort Ann.
Photo, NYS Archives

25

Upper Locks at Fort Ann.
Photo, NYS Archives

**Comstocks Landing showing hall,
general store and post office.**
Photo, Canal Society of NYS

26

Lower River Lock as it was also called, the route went across the river to the Upper River Lock. A bridge across the river at this point carried traffic, and the towpath was on the lower side. When the water was high, the boaters had the fear of the strong current pulling them down onto the dam which at that time was sometimes called the Saratoga Dam. At such time, a river stick was used. This was a piece of lumber about 1 ¼ inches thick, 5 or 6 inches wide, and about four feet long. One end was rounded to make a handle. A two inch hole was about eight inches from the other end and a tapered wooden pin about three feet long went halfway through it. This river stick was fastened about six feet behind the team. The boater had a long towline which he doubled up by putting both eyes in the ends on his cleat and the bight of the line went to the river stick. The teamster held the stick upright as it slid along the rail of the bridge, thus taking some strain off the team and also allowing the man to release the towline if there was a danger of the team being pulled backward.

The boat towed safely across the river, arrived at the Upper River Lock. The lift here was very small and the upper end had miter gates. Up until now, all the locks had a tumble gate on the upper end. This was a solid wooden gate, hinged at the bottom so that when the lock was full it could be swung outward and down to the canal bottom and the boats would float over it. It was manually cranked upright against a sill at the bottom and the walls on the sides to effectively block off the water when the lock was emptied.

Miter gates were two wooden doors, hinged at the side, which were swung to meet each other and block off the water. They were mitered so that the force of the water against them sealed them tighter. When closed, they were supported by this shape, the hinges, and the stone miter sill which the bottom of each game came to rest against. These were opened manually by pushing against a long wooden balance beam fastened to the gate and projecting out at the hinge end. The gates were not easy to open and some locktenders put down cleats for purchase for their feet as an aid in swinging them.

A two mile level brought the boat to Bassett's Lock. Here, as in some other locks, the walls had settled inward because of frost and some boats had difficulty locking through. Stonemasons were brought in and many of these locks had their walls chipped. This meant chipping some stone off the face of each wall to make the lock chamber a little wider thus doing away with the friction of the boats rubbing the walls. The added room allowed the water in the lock to run out alongside the boat which was displacing it. The upper gates leaked some and this made it very hard to pull the boat into the lock. At times, the teams had to use a block and tackle on the towline for added power to get the boats into the tight fitting lock. Other places where block lines were used were The Upper Two Lock, Hewitt's Lock, Fort Miller Lock, Moses Kill Lock, and, worst of all, The Brewery Lock at Fort Edward.

The team left Bassett's Lock and soon crossed another change bridge to the towpath on the right side. They locked up through Fort Miller Lock (miter gates) and again used a change bridge to get to the towpath now on the left side and running along the river. A narrow three mile level, with few places where loaded boats would pass each other, led to Moses Kill Lock. This one had a tumble gate. A big bend both above and below the lock made it difficult getting in or out of either end. Above the lock was an aqueduct which carried the canal over Moses Kill Creek. This hard towing level brought the boat to Fort Edward where a change bridge just before the Pottery put the towpath back on the right hand side. The level was five miles long and brought the boat to Lock #15, Fort Edward Lock, also called the Brewery Lock because of the large brewery near it. Just above this lock a little canal ran off to the left to the papermill. The entrance to this channel was blocked off by a tumble gate. Boatloads of pulpwood went into this canal under the Marbleshop bridge, to unload at the papermill. They might be seen for a mile or more, tied up to the bank, waiting to get into the waterway into the mill.

The boat was now on the summit level which was the highest in the system and fed water south to Waterford and north to Whitehall. The feedwater for this system came from the Hudson River above Glens Falls and down through the Glens Falls Feeder Canal to the Champlain. More about the Feeder in another chapter. From the Brewery Lock to the Fort Ann Locks

Old Champlain Canal, Whitehall.
Photo, NYS Archives

Whitehall, N.Y.
Photo, Canal Society of NYS

29

1900 - Whitehall harbor looking north.
Photo, Canal Society of NYS

Lake Champlain tow.
Photo, Frank Godfrey

was twelve miles. After passing the Feeder Canal, the towing was much easier because of going with the current.

When meeting other tows in the canal, the teams kept to the left side of the towpath and the boats kept to the right side of the canal. The team that was traveling with the current would stop pulling and allow the towline to sink to the bottom and the boat coming against the current would pass over it. An exception to this might be when a light boat had a side wind making it difficult to stay to his proper side and the steersman would shout, "Take the other side." Then the procedure would be reversed with the teams keeping right and the boats keeping left. When one tow passed another, the one being passed kept to the heelpath while its team kept to the right side of the towpath and stopped to let the towline sink. The overtaking team and tow passed over the towline and the passing was accomplished. When the steamboats entered the canal, they always kept to the heelpath side to avoid entangling the team's towing line in the tug's propeller.

Just past Fort Ann there were two combined locks then a short level and a single lock. These all had miter gates. After the third lock, there was another change bridge and the towpath went to the left hand side. The canal now made use of Wood Creek which, though having many bends, was easier towing because the water was deeper and wider. At a place called Flat Rock, or as the old boatmen called it, Driver's Rock, the edge of the channel was rock and straight up and down and boats could land right up against it. This was a popular spot for the boats to pull in and allow the drivers to come aboard for a meal. Also, when south-bound, to save time, the son or daughter of the boatman might drive the team the two miles to Fort Ann while the driver ate and rested and told tall stories of his early days on the canal.

Next to be encountered was Wood Lock. It dropped about five feet and had miter gates... It was not made of wood as the name implies. A little distance north of Wood Lock was a small community named Comstock. It was here that a large prison would be built. After negotiating some large bends in Wood Creek where the water was deep and wide, the boat approached a Guard Lock. This was at the entrance to a man-made artificial waterway, the canal, which led to Whitehall. The water in Wood Creek was sometimes high because of rain or melting snow in the spring. The lock protected the canal by closing the miter gates and not allowing this water to flood into it. The towpath along Wood Creek had been made very high so boats could still use this waterway but when arriving at the artificial section they had to lock down to the level of the canal. When Wood Creek was down to normal, the lock gates would both be left open, called pressed, and the boats would go right through. The little current flowing through the lock made the five mile tow to Whitehall a little easier.

Just before the Guard Lock, there was a change bridge which carried the teams over the canal to the towpath on the east side. The run to Whitehall was long and straight but there were many places where boats could not get past each other without getting aground. One tow would have to stop in a good spot and wait for the other to pass. Coal boats were always deep and often overloaded. Boats loaded with hay from Canada were not as deep and could pass with less difficulty. Lumber boats, with a high deck load of green lumber, could be deep and also rather top heavy. When towed across Lake Champlain, they were usually towed in pairs, side by side, for greater stability. There was no danger of capsizing in the canal due to its shallow depth. The bottom of the vessel would rest on the canal bed before tipping over. The canalers felt that the Champlain Canal was neglected while the Erie was made deeper and maintained far better.

On arrival at Whitehall the canal boats locked down into Lake Champlain. The Line boats usually went on the left, or west, side at The Line office and barn to await a tow leaving for Canada. Some of the Line tugs were the *Wetherbee, B.W. Burleigh, H.G. Tisdale, Protector, Defender*, and *Robert H. Cook*. Tows of 50 to 60 boats towed two abreast left each night about midnight, snubbed the tow down around The Elbow, and continued down the lake. The Union boats tied up on the right to wait for the tug *Unique* or *Peerless* towing for the Union on Lake Champlain.

Chapter 3

First Tugboat

The *Annex*
Photo, Canal Society of NYS

The first tugboat to enter a regular towing business in the Champlain Canal was said to be the *Annex*, a little vessel about 44 ft. long 12 ft. wide, and with a draft of about 4 ft. 8 inches. The engine had an eight inch bore and a nine inch stroke and was provided steam by a horizontal boiler. This little tug was built at Eddyville, near Kingston, to carry passengers and had later been a bumboat in the Poughkeepsie area of the Hudson River. It had been sunk and temporarily abandoned at Newburgh. Louis Vandervoort's father purchased the vessel, raised it, installed a new boiler, and operated it as a tugboat working out of Newburgh, Highland Falls, Rondout, and other nearby places.

A contract was obtained for the *Annex* to work for the Ticonderoga Pulp and Paper Mill so in July of 1903 she steamed up the Hudson River on the way to the job. At Waterford she picked up two boats (a double header) and towed them to White-hall. This helped defray the expenses of the trip.

The mill was at the foot of the creek where it emptied into Lake Champlain. Boats loaded with timber would drop off of the big tows and anchor in the lake. Some boats had anchors, but others might have a big rock, an old stove, or any other weight that would hold them. There might be ten or fifteen of these boats there at one time. *Annex* towed these boats in close to the mill and put the boom around them. The boom was a series of timbers loosely hooked together end to end by short lengths of chain. When a boat was safely within the confines of the boom it was unloaded. The timbers were unloaded from the boat, dropped in the water, and fed to a conveyer which took them into the mill to be cut up. At the end of the season the *Annex* ran back to Whitehall where she picked up a tow of boats loaded with potatoes from Burlington and took them to Waterford. This was the first full length towing in this canal by a tugboat.

In 1904 the *Annex* went back to Ticonderoga. She again towed two boats to Whitehall at a price of thirty dollars for each boat, worked the summer at Ti, and towed four boats down the canal in the fall. 1905 saw the same operation and the *Annex* was now regularly engaged in Champlain Canal towing.

In 1906 the Ticonderoga mill leased a little tug called the *Ti Pulp* and the *Annex* sought other work. The next year the paper mill had a new little tug built for them to tow up into Ti Creek. It was built at the Marvel Shipyard in Newburgh, N.Y. and named *C.E. Bush* after an executive of the company.

The winter of 1905-06 ice was harvested from Lake Champlain and stacked on Five Mile Point. That summer the *Annex* towed canal boats loaded with this ice from there to Whitehall where teams towed them to Waterford on the way to New York. Ice was not a common load for canal boats but when a warm winter caused a shortage of ice on the Hudson River they were pressed into service. Considerable melting occurred so the boatmen did more than the normal amount of work with the "weeping willow", otherwise known as the tin pump and springpole.

Although the *Annex* was the first tugboat to compete with horses and mules and haul boats on the Champlain Canal on a regular basis there were other earlier steam vessels. The Lake Champlain Transportation Company had a small, twin screw,

Capt. Vandervoort, owner and operator,
pulling the *Annex.*
Photo, NYS Archives

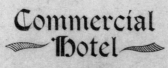

Commercial
~Hotel~

Stillwater, opposite Stillwater bridge.
T. J. JOYCE, PROP.

Hotel thoroughly renovated
Rooms well ventilated

SITUATED ON THE BANKS OF THE
HUDSON.
AN IDEAL PLACE FOR SUMMER
BOARDERS.

FINE FISHING.

GOOD LIVERY STABLE ATTACHED.
RATES $2 PER DAY.
SPECIAL RATES TO SUMMER BOARD-
ERS ON APPLICATION.
STILLWATER JOURNAL PRINT.

Time Table
SCHUYLERVILLE
STEAMBOAT COMPANY.

Steamer Bemis Heights,

April, 1897

Commercial Hotel . . . .

STILLWATER,
opposite Stillwater bridge.

T J. Joyce, Prop.
Rates $2 per day.

SPECIAL RATES to summer boarders
made known on application . .

**Schedule front. Old steamboat in Hudson River
between Schuylerville and Stillwater.**
Photo, Jim Petit

35

COMMERCIAL HOTEL, opposite the bridge, STILLWATER, N. Y.

The Schuylerville Steamboat Company,
TIME TABLE.

Steamer Bemis Heights. April 26, 1897,

Two blasts of whistle will be blown ten minutes before the boat leaves Stillwater or Schuylerville, and one blast at one minute before leaving time.

Stops on signal at Bemis Heights, Wilburs Basin, Sarles Ferry, and Coveville to take on or land passengers.

Leave	A. M.	P. M.		A. M.	P. M.	Leave	A. M.	P. M.		A. M.	P. M.
Schuy'ville	8.00	4.00		8.00	1.00	Stillwater	9.45	6.00		9.40	4.30
Coveville	8.25	4.25		8.25	1.35	Bemis Hght	10.10	6.25		10.05	4.55
Sarles Ferry	8.45	4.45	SUNDAY	8.45	1.55	Wilburs Bas	10.35	6.50	SUNDAY	10.30	5.20
Wilburs Bas	8.55	4.55		8.55	2.05	Sarles Ferry	10.45	7.00		10.40	5.30
Bemis Hght	9.15	5.15		9.15	2.30	Coveville	11.05	7.20		11.00	5.50
Stillwater *ar*	9.40	5.40		9.40	3.00	Schuy'lle *ar*	11.35	7.45		11.40	6.30

RATES OF FARE.

	Fare	R. T.			Fare	R. T.
Schuylerville to Coville, - -	15 ct.	20 ct.	Mechan'ville to Schuylerville,		50 ct.	80 ct.
" Sarles Ferry,	25 ct.	40 ct.	Stillwater to Bemis Hghts., -		10 ct.	20 ct.
" Wilburs Basin,	25 ct.	40 ct.	" Sarles Ferry, -		25 ct.	40 ct.
" Bemis Hghts.,	30 ct.	50 ct.	" Wilburs Basin, -		25 ct.	40 ct.
" Stillwater, -	40 ct.	60 ct.	" Coveville, - -		30 ct.	50 ct.
" Mechanieville,	50 ct.	80 ct.	" Schuylerville, -		40 ct.	60 ct.

Boats connect with electric cars for Mechanicville and with the D. & H. for Troy, Cohoes and Albany. J. A. POWERS, Treas. A. W. MOREY, Capt.

Schedule back. Old steamboat on Hudson River between Schuylerville and Stillwater.
Photo, Jim Petit

Tug in background is *Addie Richardson*, 2nd tug on the Champlain Canal. Abe Lent, owner.
NYS Archives

experimental vessel, meant to tow between Whitehall and Fort Edward, but it was not very successful. Capt. Frank Godfrey told of a packet boat which operated in the early 1880s. This vessel was built at Sandy Hill (Hudson Falls) and was owned by Eddie Wood. It was a small boat, smaller than a Feeder Canal boat, and built for one man operation. It had about a four ft. side and a small engine. The upright boiler and smokestack were ahead of the steersman. This little packet boat carried package freight to and from canal ports between Troy and Fort Edward. The railroad, being farther west, did not serve the communities along the river and canal so the little freighter served the purpose and was successful. When the Hudson Valley Railway established its trolley line between Troy and Fort Edward it ran near these canal communities. This took business from the packet boat and caused its demise.

In 1897 the Schuylerville Steamboat Company operated the steamer *Bemis Heights* between Schuylerville and Stillwater but I think this was on the Hudson River.

The second tugboat to operate in the Champlain Canal was said to be the *Addie Richardson*, owned and operated by Abe "Dirty Dick" Lent and his son.

Means of steering a double-header.
Photo, Fred Godfrey

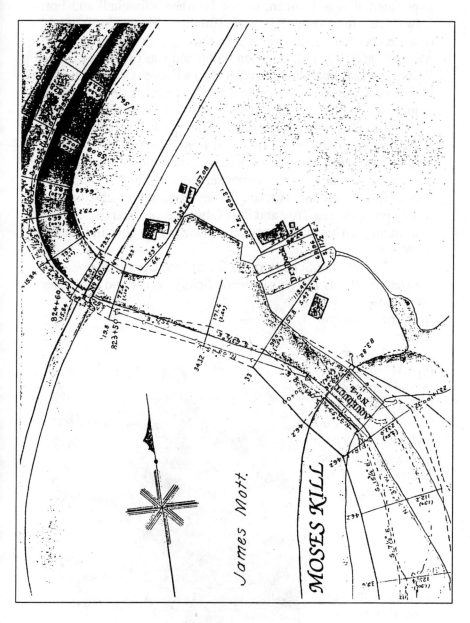

Moses Kill Lock

Chapter 4

Tugboat Tow

A tug towing a double header or two double headers would take about five days of 15-16 hours each to travel 62 miles from Waterford to Whitehall. With a small tow, long hours, and a lot of luck, the trip could be made in four days. The teams towed only one boat at a time and made better time than the tugs, especially going upstream. The steam whistle was seldom used to notify a lock that a tug was coming. They traveled at such a slow speed that the locktender usually saw them and had the lock ready. Some, not all, of the canal boats using animals had a horn for signaling. Louis said they did not need a horn because most of them had "long distance voices."

The little tugboats of that day carried a crew of three. Captain, Fireman-Engineer, and Deckhand-Cook. Deckhand's pay was $15 per month and the other two received $60 each. The captain steered the boat, occasionally helped the deckhand, handled the money, and was in charge of the operation. The engineer operated and maintained the engine and kept steam in the boiler. The deckhand shined brass, kept the ship clean, took on coal, dumped the ashes in the canal (which was illegal), steered a little so the captain could rest, cooked the meals, and had other strenuous duties which will be described later. Living conditions were very primitive. A wooden locker contained canned goods, a few articles of clothing and a pallet on top for sleeping. There was no refrigeration, no electricity, and no window screens to keep out insects. Mosquitoes feasted on the men who were sleeping soundly after a long workday. Washing facilities did not exist. Water was carried in a barrel for drinking and cooking but the rest was bailed from the canal with a bucket on a rope. It was many years later before these conditions were improved upon to any great degree.

A typical "good trip" of four days from Waterford to Whitehall with a double header would get underway about four A.M. after a big breakfast. The deckhand, of course, had to be up early to provide this meal, even though he might have been up all night playing poker in the weighlock building. A fast trip meant more money for the boatmen in the tow, so they would throw stones at the tug to wake up the crew if an early start was not underway. They would be very angry also if they were tied up too long at night. They liked to see the tugs have a workday twenty hours long. Tie up the first night would be at Baker's Lock between Mechanicville and Stillwater. This route was over a two mile level, three mile level, one mile level, and a four mile level — ten miles and five locks in 16 hours.

Food was plentiful but fresh meat was scarce. Refrigeration was unknown, and these little tugs did not have ice boxes at that time. "Canalers Fresh meat" was ham. Approaching Mechanicville, northbound, the captain would swing the tug in to the towpath so the deckhand could jump off and run ahead. He would buy 5 loaves of bread for $.25 and a couple pounds of fresh meat for $.25 and then get back on the tug.

Day two again started very early in the morning. The tug and tow now must lock up through Baker's Lock. This is work, particularly for the deckhand. When the tug and tow approached a lock, the canaler, when he thought he had enough headway, shouted "all right" and threw off the hawser which the deckhand coiled up on the stern. The tug entered the lock and the canalboat captain threw a line over a post and snubbed the boat to a stop below the lock. The locktender closed the lower gates, closed the paddles which had let the water out, and walked to the upper end of the lock. Here the paddles were opened and when the lock was full the gates were opened or, as in this case being a tumble gate, it was dropped. The tug ran out fifty feet above the lock and the captain put a line on a post to hold it there. The deckhand ran as fast as he could with a towline over his shoulder, extending this line from the tug the full length of the lock. The lower end of the lock had a foot bridge across from wall to wall and the line had

1910 - Waterford, N.Y.
Photo, Canal Society of NYS

**Waterford, N.Y. - Frank Godfrey in rowboat.
Two boats on far right are *Archer* and *Yell*
owned by Godfrey family.**
Photo, Canal Society of NYS

Waterford side cut.
Photo, Frank Godfrey

Weighlock at Waterford looking south.
Photo, NYS Archives

Mechanicvile, N.Y.
Photo, NYS Archives

**Lock #13, Fort Miller, Sam Shepard crossing gate.
Note levers for opening valves.**
Photo, Jim Petit

43

Sanders Boatyard
Photo, Jim Petit

Moses Kill at Patterson's Store looking south.
Photo, Jim Petit

44

to go under this bridge and to the canal boat. The deckhand flipped the end of the line down under the bridge and caught the eye that was spliced in its end on the toe of his shoe. He then pulled the line down to the boatman who put it on his bow bitts or cleat. Meantime, the locktender had been dumping the lock. The deckhand ran back up to the tug to care for the towline and when the gates were opened the tug pulled the first boat into the lock. The second boat cut loose and stopped below the lock as had the first one. Now the man on the boat entering the lock must put out a line to stop his boat from hitting the miter sill and immediately put out another line to keep his boat from drifting back out of the lock. If this happened, the tug had to again pull the boat back into the lock so the gates could be closed. The locktender now raised the boat up as before and opened the gate. Now the tug, which was the length of the towline up the canal, backed down to about fifty feet from the lock as the deckhand pulled in the towline. The tug could not come any closer because the propeller might wash gravel or whatever else might be on the canal bottom into the miter sill. If debris was against the sill, the gate couldn't be closed until it was removed. The tug now towed the boat up the canal for three or four hundred feet with the boatman steering it with his rudder. When the boat had sufficient headway, the tug backed down past the barge and the deckhand flipped the line off of the horn of the cleat. A good boatman might steer in close to the towpath and put a line around a tree or telegraph pole to hold him there. When the tug was again fifty feet above the lock, a bow line was again put out and the deckhand again ran down the lock to repeat the whole procedure. This was done for each boat in the tow until all were locked up, coupled together, and the tug took them in tow.

The locktender on Baker's Lock would be offered $.25 to keep the wickets on the spillway closed as long as possible. This stopped the current in the canal, raised the water level, and made it much easier for the tug. Not a bad investment for the tug owner. Locking down was much easier. A $.25 tip to the lock operator made a big difference. The tug entered the lock and the tow stopped above the lock close to the gates. The steamboat locked down and tied up below the lock. When the lock was again filled and the upper gates open, the locktender would go to the lower end of the lock and open the paddles. This caused a little current to flow through the lock and pulled the first boat in while the others cut off above the lock. The locktender then closed the paddles, went to the upper end, closed the gates and proceeded on with the locking procedure. When the lock was empty, with the gates open, the tug put a line on the boat and pulled it out of the lock where the boatman caught a line on a post and held it while waiting for the next boat. This was repeated until all of the fleet was locked down. It's remarkable what $.25 would buy. Captain Bob Leddick said they would offer a driver ten cents to try to pass another boat. He said for ten to twenty-five cents they would build a house for you. An obvious exaggeration but it indicates the value of money in those days.

A run of sixteen miles over "the long level" brought the tow to Schuylerville. The usual work of going through the lock at Schuylerville, and then the tug pulled the tow across the river at Northumberland, entered the canal and tied up for the night at the Upper River Lock. When at Schuylerville, the tug might be "coaled up" at Funston's Coal Yard. Hard coal was used and the yard owner would have canvas bags of pea coal setting on the dock. Three to four tons would be needed and often the canalers would help with this chore in order to save time. They were always in a hurry and unwilling to stop. In later days the tugs burned soft coal because it was cheaper but it was a lot dirtier.

Day three brought another difficult long day's work. A two mile level, and a one mile level to Fort Miller Lock where Mrs. Sanders sold layer cakes for $.25 and delicious pies for $.20. From Fort Miller to Moses Kill was three miles and on to Fort Edward was five miles more. That last five miles was very hard towing. There was a little white-bearded man who lived near the towpath and he was a Bank Watcher. As the names implies, he watched the canal banks for leaks and controlled the wickets on the waste weir to keep the water level constant. he would walk alongside the tug but say not a word. The Captain would toss him a quarter saying, "Buy yourself a cigar." The man would walk back to his house and would not open a wicket to lower the water level. His unspoken threat was not needed...A quarter was a good

**Tows meeting at Patterson's feeding place.
Tug *Thomas Miller,* Capt. Bert Lee,
Engineer Bill Vandervoort, Deckhand George Lord.**
Photo, Canal Society of NYS

Aqueduct at Moses Kill.
Photo, Jim Petit

47

**View south from Notre Dame St. bridge,
Fort Edward.**
Photo, NYS Archives

Chaplain Canal at Fort Edward.
Photo, Canal Society of NYS

48

**Feeder to the paper mill at
Fort Edwward about 1910.**
Photo, NYS Archives

Tug *Lillian* at Fort Ann locks.
Photo, Canal Society of NYS

Whitehall, N.Y.
Photo, NYS Archives

Whitehall, N.Y.
Photo, NYS Archives

investment. The canal had been cut through shale rock and sometimes when the lock at Moses Kill was filled it drew the water down so that deeply laden boats sat on the bottom until the backswell from the lock allowed them to go on. Twenty-five cents to a bank watcher paid off. Eight hours over this five miles was considered good time.

The tug and tow entered Fort Edward, went through the aqueduct, under Notre Dame St. bridge, past the New York State Shops on the left, under East St. bridge, and arrived at the Brewery Lock. It was hard to pull boats into this lock and a block line was often used but with the usual hard work and a little extra effort they were locked up. Above the lock, the towing was again rather hard because of the canalboats tied up for about a mile on the west bank of the canal. They were loaded with pulp wood from Canada and were waiting to go through the little branch canal to the papermill at Fort Edward. Once past this area, the tow soon arrived at the outlet of the Glens Falls Feeder Canal which supplied the water for the Champlain Canal. Now on the summit lever, with water flowing south to Waterford and north to Whitehall, the towing became much easier. At the end of the third hard day, the tow tied up at Smith's Basin.

Day four was better. After the usual early start and a fairly easy run with the current, Fort Ann was reached. Here there were three locks: two combines, a short level, and a single lock. A man named Ike Terry, with a team of mules, charged $.50 per boat to lock them through all three locks. A man and a team of mules for $.50! This saved wear and tear on the tug and also allowed the crew to get some rest. The rest of the day was spent going to Wood Lock, through the easy towing waters of Wood Creek, through the Guard Lock, and on to Whitehall where the big tows of The Line left for ports on Lake Champlain and Canada. The hawser was released from the boats which drifted down to the triple locks and were pulled through them by mules to exit into the lake. At times, the little canal tug might work twenty-four hours straight in order to reach Whitehall in time for the boats to make the big tow. This also meant that the tug could hook onto a southbound tow earlier.

51

Some typical towing rates of that time:

Waterford to Whitehall,
      . . . . . . Loaded boat $30
      . . . . . . Light boat $15
Whitehall to Waterford,
      . . . . . . Loaded lumber boat $25
      . . . . . . Hay boat $18
      . . . . . . Light boat $12

The crew had completed a four day trip which could have taken a day longer. Delays could have been encountered at locks when arriving at the same time as other units. Boats might have been wedged in tight locks or wedged in the canal when meeting other boats.

This was an opportunity for the men to get a good meal. There were lunch wagons on the heel path of the canal from the coal yard to the foot bridge and one on a side street, near Mansville's Drug Store. The food was delicious to the men who had been eating well but often in haste and without fresh meat and fresh milk. The captain would now go to the office of The Inland Seaman's Union, which was over the drug store, and arrange for a southbound tow.

Locks at Whitehall.
Photo, NYS Archives

Whitehall Harbor
Photo, NYS Archives

53

***Defender* at Rouses Pt.**
Photo, Frank Godfrey

Winter, Whitehall, N.Y.
Photo, Canal Society of NYS

Chapter 5

Business

The Champlain Canal was the main artery for commerce in northeastern New York and many businesses flourished along its banks. There were many saloons along the route, a few of which had good entertainment. Small grocery stores were there to provide the boatmen and families with food. Some general stores had large inventories and could provide anything needed or desired. William Nealer ran The Inland Seamen's store at the Weighlock. He also bought and sold some of the coal lightered off the boats.

Understandably, there were many boatyards to provide repairs and to build new boats. One that is better known than others because it lasted longer is John E. Matton's formerly operated by his father Jesse Matton. This yard was located on the west side of the canal just above the Upper Two Lock at Waterford. A basin which had been dug out alongside the canal operated very much like a lock. A tumble gate separated the canal from the basin and when the basin was filled with water from the canal the tumble gate was dropped and the boat needing repairs was floated in. The tumble gate was raised, the water drained, and the boat could then be worked on. Many canal boats were built there at a cost of about $3,500.00 each in 1910. Before that time he built the *Alice E. Brodie*, named after my grandmother, and her pride and joy. Unfortunately, she retired and went ashore before I became of an age to remember the boat except in pictures.

John E. Matton was a hard worker, as was his wife. In the evening they could be seen sitting on the canal bank, wearing leather aprons, and rolling oakum on their laps. Oakum was composed of old fibers such as hemp and was used for caulking seams between planks on the boats. This material came in bales and rolling it, or "spinning oakum" as it was commonly called, was the process by which the material was made into a string-like shape and wound into balls to be used by the caulkers. The thickness of the string depended upon the size of the seam to be caulked. The workman would force the oakum into the seam using a caulking iron (much like a cold chisel but with a very wide blade) and a caulking mallet. The sound of a caulking (they would pronounce it corkin') hammer at work was very distinctive. It was a very high pitched "cleak" and so different from other shipyard sounds that one always knew if the "corkers" were working.

John E. Matton moved his operations to the west bank of the Hudson River below Waterford. Here he prospered with a floating dry dock, a repair yard, a fleet of tugboats, and a least one oil barge, the *Jemson #1*. His son Ralph joined him in the business and they built many steel tugs, oil barges, and many other craft.

The following shows how John Matton kept close tabs on the expenses of operating his business. In 1932 I spent my summer vacation from high school assisting my father who was Marine Superintendent for Lake Champlain Despatch Company and Murray Transportation Company with an office at 120th Street North Troy. I answered the telephone, typed letters, sent daily reports to the New York office, and cared for the place when my dad was out. The good part for me was that I occasionally spent some time "hamming" on one of the tugs. One day Mr. Matton phoned my father. He started with a strange question.

"George, how many sheets of toilet paper do you use when you take a shit?"

No definite answer was received to his question so he went on to say that his tugboats were using too much toilet tissue. He had taken the number of men in a crew, the number of times he estimated they visited the head, counted the number of sheets in a roll, and came up with a result showing a very large number of sheets used per person. He suspected the crew was stealing his paper and he was probably right. I do not know what action was taken.

At Flynn's Lock was a grocery store and it also contained an illegal still. The operator was William Smith from Kingston,

John E. Matton
Photo, Frank Godfrey

**Matton boatyard, Champlain Canal.
Barge and houseboat underconstruction.**
Photo , Canal Society of NYS

**Standard Wallpaper Co., Liberty Branch
Schuylerville, NY**
Photo, NYS Archives

**Bridge over Hudson River at Northumberland.
Canal boats are at boatyard of Jesse Billings.**
Photo, Canal Society of NYS

N.Y. The product of the still was used by some of the canalers and teamsters. A boat owner with a single boat might hire a steersman to help him by steering a trick through the canal. If the owner had a double header he would need the man to steer and to care for the second boat. The steersman could be picked up at Waterford for an up tow and at Whitehall for a down tow. Many of them were an irresponsible lot interested in working only enough to survive and have the price of a drink. When aboard a boat they were fed by the owner and would recover somewhat from the latest binge but, when discharged, would head for the nearest saloon. If they could wheedle some cash out of the boat owner they would buy the product of the illegal still, much to the chagrin of the boat owner.

One mile northward was Hewitt's Lock where George Reed was locktender on one shift. He operated a little grocery store with no drinks except soft stuff.

At Mechanicville the West Virginia Pulp and Paper Company operated along the canal and later received shipments of pulpwood and fuel oil along the Hudson River when the Barge Canal came into being. Moulding sand and clay bricks were also shipped from Mechanicville.

At Baker's Lock Bill Severence ran a real saloon with entertainment imported from New York City. He had girls who danced on the tables and, it is hinted, performed other services. Severence was described as a nice fellow, very outgoing, a big man, always with a big cigar in his mouth, a dandy, a real sport, and a patron of the cock fights held in Glens Falls and Fort Edward.

There was a Line barn at Baker's Lock, the first one since the one at Waterford. Here the driver would be instructed by the barn boss (and dispatcher) as to his duties. He might be replaced by another team and driver, or if none was available, he would rest six hours and go on. He usually stayed with the same team but sometimes, after a lay-off for rest or lack of work, he would be given a different set of mules. If the team was wanted somewhere else the driver would be sent on with them. This was called "leading up" and, as nothing was being towed, the six hour stop for rest was deemed not necessary.

A story was told of a teamster for The Line who was a real drunk and who liked to stop in at Bill Severence's saloon. One dark, rainy night he drank to his capacity and passed out. The Line boss, assisted by another man, threw the teamster onto the back of the lead mule, a leg on each side and his arm pits hooked over the hames. The lead mule, and the rest of the string, was started on its way with the unconscious passenger in the pouring rain. As far as is known they all arrived safely at Schuylerville 16 miles farther on.

The lead mule on a line team was an intelligent animal and there was no fear of it going into the canal. The reins ran from the driver to each animal up to the lead mule but he seldom used them. He might go to the first animal an take hold of its head to turn the team around but most of the time the lead mule did the piloting. Very few teamsters abused the mules but the work was very hard on the animals especially when towing loaded boats. In winter the mules were often boarded out to people who had the use of them in return for their feeding and care. The care was sometimes not very good.

About one half mile above Baker's Lock, on the west side, was another little dry dock, owner's name not remembered.

Part way over this sixteen mile level was Wilbur's Basin, sometimes called Van Wie's. This was a spot where teams used to stop to feed and water and take a brief rest before proceeding on. Just north of Wilbur's Basin was Searle's Ferry where sand was shipped out. Another cargo shipped from here was said to be manure for the mushroom plants on the Hudson River. I can't imagine a boat owner wanting to take such a load. In later years sand was shipped from both of these places on the Champlain Barge Canal. Farther on at Salisbury's, Surrogate Ostrander of Schuylerville had some big barns. He raised prize bulls. North of Salisbury's, past the haystack bridge, was Costello's saloon, right on the towpath. It seems that the predominate business along the canal was saloon keeping, and I feel sure they were well patronized by boatmen, drivers and steersmen, but there were probably many other businesses that flourished along the waterway that are lost to memory.

**Fort Edward Brewery above Lock #15.
Built in 1858-59, first brew Nov. 1859.
George H. Taylor, principal owner.**
Photo, NYS Archives.

**Hotel on west branch of old Champlain Canal
at Comstock, NY.**
Photo, Canal Society of NYS

**Jack Ryan's boatyard
Whitehall, NY**
Photo, NYS Archives

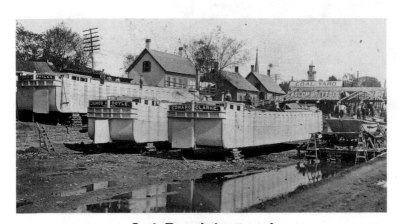

**Jack Ryan's boatyard
Whitehall, NY**
Photo, Canal Society of NYS

After leaving Costello's the next little community was Coveville. Here there was a little store and a storehouse where they used to unload coal and other cargo from the boats. A man named Millett ran a saloon there. It featured a pool table and the local farm people were very adept at shooting pool. Fishing was very good in the cove off of the river. A short distance farther on was a little place called The Hemlocks. There was no lock there but a little grocery store did a good business. The Victors was the next place reached. It was near Victory Mills. At the Victory Mills bridge there was a little sign saying that "Here General Burgoyne surrendered to General Gates." It was there for many years but was later moved to another place.

Entering Schuylerville a little dry dock was on the left hand side. This was run by Jud Whaley of Fort Edward and later by George "Boney" Sanders of Moses Kill. Just above the Ferry Street bridge was Funston Bros. Coal Yard. Canvas bags of pea coal were lined up along this dock and tugs would coal up there. Three to four tons would be taken aboard. The boat owners, always in a hurry, would sometimes help with this chore to save time. Standard Wallpaper had its large Liberty Plant in Schuylerville near the canal.

Northumberland was the next community. Here a man named Jesse Billings also built and repaired boats. He was a wealthy man who also owned a coal yard, grocery store, saloon, tenant houses, and a bank. The bank building still stands on the west side of Route #4 just south of the bridge over the Hudson River. It is easily identified as the brick building with the word bank on its facade. Al Vandervoort said that he got the last $5.00 check from that bank when he was engineer on the tug *James K. Averill* with Captain Dave Roberts. Billings had two ice houses below Schuylerville from which he shipped ice to New York City. Besides building new boats, he also traded in old canal boats. A young lad, anxious to go into business for himself, could buy an old boat for fifty to one hundred dollars down and Billings would finance the rest. It would take a lot of hard work and many hours at the old tin pump before the lad would finally get out of debt. It was expected that all boat owners, farmers, or others who were indebted to Billings would trade at his businesses.

63

Herb Beatty of Glens Falls bought his first boat, the *Thomas Gilchrist* for fifty dollars. (Not from Billings). It was in bad shape so he had to stay in the shallow water of the canal. It was traded off for a gold watch to a man who wanted it for a fishing boat. His next boat cost one hundred dollars. Then he bought the *Annie K.* for three hundred dollars. He ran this boat for three or four years. It was tied up for the winter and he was not living aboard so it was stolen. He never recovered it.

There was a saloon on the Lower River Lock at Schuyler-ville and a saloon on the Upper River Lock across the river. Two miles farther north, at Bassett's Lock, was a saloon which looked like those shown in old western movies. It was a long, low, shack with a wooden canopy across the front, and less than a foot off the towpath. A story was told of a Line driver called Stonewall Jackson. He was a big man, big voice, hands like hams, and was feared by many. He drove his four string of Line mules right into the saloon and said, "Set 'em up for the boys." The "boys", or mules were not served. They were removed from the premises but no one attempted to eject the driver.

Pulp wood was unloaded at a little basin below Fort Miller for use in the papermill. There was also a grocery store at Fort Miller Lock. Will Patterson operated a grocery store near Moses Kill Lock. In the late 1930s I used to rent a rowboat there for one dollar and spend the day fishing. Before that time people would rent a rowboat on a Sunday and have a pleasant day and a picnic on the river. The building still stands but is now a private home.

There was an old dry dock on the heelpath (east) side of the canal owned by "Boney Sanders." A tug was once drydocked there and the seams around the bow were caulked and the charge was only eight dollars. In later years he operated a dry dock at Schuylerville.

North of Moses Kill the canal was cut through shale rock and it was rather narrow with sides that were straight up and down. The boats could go close to the side allowing the owner to step onto the towpath. He would walk up to the fine canal grocery store operated by Sadler (or Satterlee), get his groceries and get back on his boat along the canal or from a bridge.

Entering Fort Edward the canal went past The Pottery which was at the corner of Broadway and Argyle Street. A large gristmill was next on the left. It has been converted to an apartment house. The canal went under the Notre Dame Street bridge, and past the large brick school house on the left. Above this was the New York State repair yard where their marine equipment was kept and maintained. From here through the East Street bridge along Spruce Street many boats were loaded and unloaded.

At one time a small Italian bakery was operated along the towpath. A big round loaf of this bread and a 5 cent can of Van Camp's beans was considered a fine treat by the boatmen passing through.

The International Paper Company had a big mill in Fort Edward and pulpwood was brought to it by boat through its own little canal which branched off from the Champlain above Lock #15 and ran into the mill. As a boy I lived in Fort Edward and, even though a descendant of a canal boat family, I did not know of this canal going into the papermill. I found out from my grandmother who often spoke of the Marbleshop bridge. When asked where it had been she told me the bridge carried traffic on Broadway across the little canal part way up Fort Edward Hill.

Alongside Fort Edward Lock was a dry dock operated by Jud Whaley who also operated a dry dock in Schuylerville at another time. This lock, Lock #15, the Brewery Lock, had a real saloon. It was run by Gus Regner, the same man who, after the opening of the Barge Canal, had a houseboat set up on the approach wall of Lock #7 and operated a small grocery store in it. I knew Mr. Regner and after his death I bought his tool chest and some of his tools. Later the saloon was operated by Mr. Williams who had three lovely daughters. It was a great saloon and the three girls made it even more attractive so sometimes the tows dallied there.

Above Lock #15 was the brewery which gave the lock its name. This operation was closed down with the coming of Prohibition. Later in that period it was operated illegally until caught and shut down by the authorities. It burned down later for a total loss. Along this summit level were potato farms and storage buildings to hold potatoes until they were loaded into boats for shipment to New York City. The Keenan Lime Company shipped their product in boats on the canal.

At Smith's Basin there was a large general store where one could buy almost anything, as Louis said, "from a needle to an anchor." It was in potato country yet he once tried to buy some potatoes and found they had none.

At Fort Ann locks there was Smith's store on the left, which Al Vandervoort said was a "regular Montgomery Ward type store" where one could buy whatever was needed. Above the second lock Sheldon's Dry Dock was on the right. Below these locks there was a knitting mill which employed about one hundred girls. They would shout to the boatmen and tell them to tie up and make a date with them.

At Comstock there was a large boarding house. Beyond Comstock, at Smith's landing, there was another. Today they would be called resort hotels. People came there to rest, commune with Nature, and escape the hectic life of the big city.

Just before entering Whitehall, on the left, was Ryan's Boatyard. It had no dry dock but winched boats up onto the launching ways when they needed repairs. The Jack Ryan boat was strong, well built, and probably the best of the Northern canal boats. It was easily recognized in the the Champlain Canal because of its distinctive bow which was much like a laker on the Erie. Unlike some of its competitors, it could be used in New York harbor in winter because of its strength and sound construction. Herb Beatty said that in 1905 a brand new Jack Ryan boat cost two to three thousand collars. Other boats could carry a little more cargo because of their lighter build. The goal was to carry 180 tons in the canal. some owners bragged that their boats could do this but, if so, they were probably loaded 5 ft. instead of the legal depth of 4 ½ ft. and the team or the little tug towing them suffered because of it.

The Ryan boats had high sides and when light in the canal would not clear some of the bridges so water would be put into the boat to sink it lower. There being no bulkheads to control it, the water ballast would roll around and cause the boat to tilt one way or another. If this happened when going under a bridge the cabin roof was damaged. The ballast water was taken on through

66

a hole in the bottom, either in the bow or the stern. When not in use this hole was sealed by a piece of wood, whittled round on one end, and driven into the hole. A board was fastened across the plug to prevent it from working loose. The water was removed by use of the tin pump and springpole, also known as the "weeping willow".

John Ryan's coal yard was north of the boatyard. That was a different man from the boatyard owners.

The large silk mill, on the east side of the lake just north of the locks employed many girls. They would call out to the boatmen, sometimes offering to make dates with them. Whether they were serious or not, I do not know.

The booming village of Whitehall was the northern terminus of the old Champlain Canal, and had stores, mills, hotels, taverns, as well as shipbuilding and other industry. The two Vandervoort brothers called Whitehall the metropolis of the north. They said the styles were in Whitehall, as in New York City, direct from Paris. The inhabitants of this quiet village are proud of their history and look back on this period with nostalgia.

Champlain Canal, Whitehall, NY
Photo, Frank Godfrey

Glens Falls Feeder Canal, 5 comboined locks
Photo, NYS Archives

Lock #1, Sept. 26, 1906
Photo, NYS Archives

Combined locks #2 and #3, Sept. 26, 1906
Photo, NYS Archives

Chapter 6

Feeder Canal

The Glens Falls Canal, as its name implies, brought water from the Hudson River above Glens Falls to the Champlain Canal. This water was fed into the canal system, flowing south to Fort Edward and north to Fort Ann. It was (and is) 7 miles long with 13 locks, the most spectacular of which are the Five Combines at its lower end. Many industries flourished along its banks and it is primarily responsible for the growth of Glens Falls and Sandy Hill (Hudson Falls). Many commodities were shipped such as lumber, limestone, paper, wall paper, cement, and others. The fee for towing from Glens Falls to Waterford was $13.00 and from Waterford to Glens Falls $18.00.

Sandy Hill, NY
Photo, NYS Archives.

Glens Falls Feeder Lock #4, Sept. 26, 1906
Photo, NYS Archives.

By-pass at Lock #10 for Locks #6 to #10, 11/12, 1907
Photo, NYS Archives.

Lock #11, Sept. 11, 1906
Photo, NYS Archives.

Feeder Canal boats were smaller than those of the Champlain Canal. They were about 90 ft. long, 13 ½ ft. wide, and of varying heights from 5 ½ to 8 ft. Northern boats were about 98 ft. long and 18 ft. wide. Because of their smaller size and lighter weight, the feeder boats were easier to tow and made better time than others. As Louis Vandervoort said, "The Glens Fallers were fast goers. They had been known to go from Glens Falls to Albany in one day—a nice long twenty hour day." He also said they hated the tugboats because of delays caused by them. Louis had respect for the Glens Fallers. "They were good men, big men, some great fighters. They took no back talk from any New Yorkers." Another man Louis respected for his fighting prowess was Hank Wait, locktender on Bassett's Lock. he was a mild mannered small man, well built and muscular, probably from work on a farm. A big Glens Falls boater pulled up to the lock and was told to move because he was blocking traffic. The big boatman refused and added some profanity and derogatory remarks. Hank Wait went down to convince the man that he must move and was back in five minutes with everything settled. The little lock keeper was unruffled but the big boatman was, as Louis put it, "All cut up. Hank trimmed him like a Christmas tree." Apparently this Feeder boatman had better success against New Yorkers than against local talent.

I can remember the bridges across the Feeder Canal at Notre Dame St. and East St. in Fort Edward. They were high above the level of the streets and needed a ramp at each end to allow traffic to cross. On Notre Dame Street, one may see a house with a door opening form the second story. This once was a level with the high approach to the bridge. Sometime later, perhaps around 1930, mechanically operated lift bridges were installed. This allowed removal of the ramps and the bridges were now at the same level as the street. I never saw one of these bridges opened. Some years later these bridges were removed and the canal filled in.

According to the 1941 annual report of The New York State Department of Public Works traffic on the Feeder "practically ceased in 1931" and was officially closed for navigation on April, 1941.

Glens Falls Feeder, Lock #12, Sept. 11, 1906, *Photo, NYS Archives*

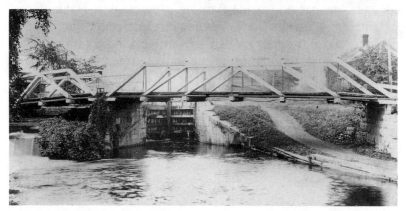

Lock #13 and Pearl St. Bridge, Sept. 11, 1906, *Photo, NYS Archives*

Martindale Bridge at Sandy Hill, Sept. 11, 1906 *Photo, NYS Archives*

I have a slight connection with the Glens Falls Feeder Canal. My great grandfather, when very old, was locktender on the Junction Lock at Fort Edward near the end of its operation.

My father, when eighteen years old, ran a pair of boats for the Griffin Lumber Co. He had been warned by the yard men that one of Griffin's drivers, a man named Ed Combs, always brought bad reports back to Griffin about whatever happened on the trip. The boatmen preferred other drivers. When the two boats were loaded, my dad asked for a driver and requested Ed Combs. In the morning, the team was hitched to the tow cart (Ed could not walk very well) and they headed south with the tow. On the way down, they stopped late at night at Baker's Lock where Bill Severance ran a saloon complete with dancing girls and all amenities for the entertainment of hard working men. My father and his steersman went with the teamster and helped care for the team and then persuaded him to go with them to the saloon. he went there and had a wonderful time throwing away his money on drinks and women. In the early morning, they had great difficulty awakening him but finally succeeded in getting him on his cart and getting under way.

George Godfrey with Griffin Lumber boat.
Photo, Fred Godfrey

73

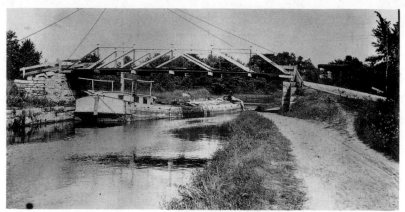

Glens Falls Feeder, County Line Bridge, Sept. 11, 1906
Photo, NYS Archives

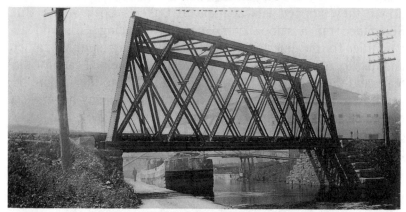

D. & H. R.R. Bridge Cement Co. footbridge
Sept. 11, 1906   *Photo, NYS Archives*

Waste Weir, Sept. 11, 1906, *Photo, NYS Archives.*

74

Upon arrival at Waterford, the boats were to continue on to New York and the team return to Sandy Hill. The teamster was broke, having spent all of his money and also the money allotted him by Griffins to buy feed or the team. He asked my father if he could borrow some money from him to tide him over. "Sure," said Dad. "How much do you want?" The amount was soon agreed upon and my father asked, "Shall I turn the bill in to Griffins?"

"No! Oh no! I'll pay you when you get back."

Later on when the boats, loaded with coal, returned to Griffins, the yardmen wanted to know what had been done to Ed Combs. They said that when the driver returned, he reported that George Godfrey was the only real man that ever was on those boats. Many years later, that young boy boatman, when retired from work, enjoyed talking with Laurence Griffin about the role of the Griffin Lumber Co. on the feeder.

The Glens Falls Feeder Canal Society has done a fine job of cleaning up the canal and promoting it as a great historical and recreational resource.

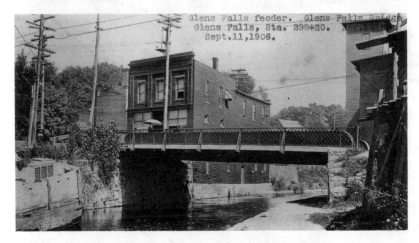

Glens Falls Feeder, foot of Glen St.
Sept. 11, 1906 *Photo, NYS Archives*

Glens Falls Feeder, Bridge at Pruyn Lime Kiln, Sept. 11, 1906
Photo, NYS Archives

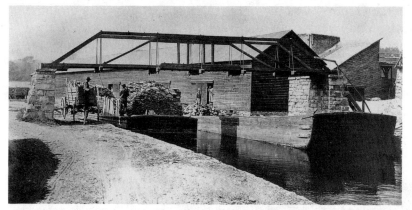

Foot bridge over Glens Falls Feeder, Sept. 11, 1906 *Photo, NYS Archives*

Feeder Canal above Glens Falls, *Photo, NYS Archives*

Last load on Glens Falls Feeder.
Paper from Finch Pruyn, Glens Falls.
Photo, Jim Petit

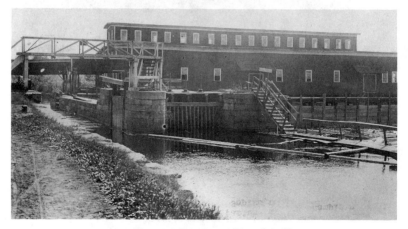

Guard Lock at Feeder Dam
Sept. 11, 1906
Photo, NYS Archives

Vandervoort Houseboat
Mother, Julia and daughter, Beatrice.
Photo, Bea Coolidge.

Probably the Vandervoort family.
Photo, Canal Society of NYS.

Chapter 7

Houseboat

The power to move the vessels and their cargoes on the old Champlain Canal was provided by mules, horses, and also, starting in 1903, by little tugboats. In July 1910, a different type of vessel was towed through the canal by two men, with some help.

Al Vandervoort owned a houseboat named *Rudder Grange*. It was fifty-five ft. long, 16 ½ ft. wide, with a 4 ft. side and a draft of one foot and, to use their words. "A beautiful little home, all modern." The houseboat was to go to Ticonderoga so Al and his brother Louis decided it would be a good idea for them to pull her up the canal themselves. They left the Weighlock, July 1, 1910 at 4:00 a.m. with the two brothers acting as mules and their mother, Julia steering the boat with an oar over the stern. Other members of the family were passengers and included little sister Beatrice, Al's wife Mary, and son Allie.

One mile up the ditch, they locked through the Lower Two Lock where the locktenders were men named McLaughlin, Socks Smith, and Eddie Welch of coal yard fame. One quarter mile farther on they went through the Upper Two Lock where Frank Bosely was locktender. John E. Matton later built a boat for him and he went boating. He had enough of being paid $40.00 for a month of 12 hour days.

After dragging the houseboat three miles to Flynn's Lock, the two human mules realized that they had tackled a job that was all work. To make matters worse, the weather was unseasonably hot and they suffered because of it. Wickham Smith was lock tender here and lived in a house right on the towpath. He made moonshine for sale to the passers-by. This same man came from Kingston and had helped build the *Annex* in Eddyville.

A hard, hot drag of one mile brought them to Hewitt's Lock. George Reed, locktender, had operated a grocery store which he sold to Leggett, another locktender. Leggett had three pretty daughters Lizzie, Mary, and Agnes.

Upon arrival at Mechanicville lift bridge a stop was made for supper and a little rest. Mother, Mary, and the kids went to the movies at the theater on the heel path just above the bridge. The two brothers "went to town and licked up some delicious ice cream sodas." Being refreshed, they started up again and got up to the West Virginia Pulp Wood railroad bridge to find the canal blocked by some pulpwood boats above the bridge. Al went up to the canal boat and receiving no answer to his shouts went down into the cabin. Here he found Hank Mansfield half drunk, sitting and eating by the light of a smoked up lantern. Al asked him to move so the houseboat could get past. The reply was that he wouldn't move for anybody. Al said that if he didn't come out he would be dragged out. The boatman decided to come out under his own power and the boat was moved to allow the houseboat to proceed on. They tied up at Baker's Lock a half hour past midnight after a long, hard, hot, day of work.

July 2, 1910, started out at 5 a.m. after "a good nights sleep" (their words, not mine). At Stillwater bend, the women went to the stores and caught up to the boat by the car barns. It was another hot day with temperatures in the nineties, and they were on the long sixteen mile level. While stopped for lunch and a brief rest, John Munson came down past with the tug *Lillian* and two lumber boats. He shouted over, "When I come back I'll pick you up and tow you to Whitehall." They started again and got up as far as Wilbur's Basin, when the tug *William P. Dalton*, with four coal boats, overtook them. Their older brother, Elmer Vandervoort, was engineer on the *Dalton*. The houseboat was hooked on the back of the tow and towed through Schuylerville, through the Lower River Lock at Northumberland, across the North River, to the Upper River Lock. It was 8 p.m. and the tug tied up for the night. Elmer changed his clothes and helped haul the houseboat over the two mile level to Bassett's Lock. He then

80

had a two mile walk back to his job on the tug, and this was after working a long day as fireman and engineer on the tugboat.

The towing team, again reduced to two humans, hauled their tow the one mile to Fort Miller. This place was famous along the canal as the place where Mrs. Sanders sold four-layer cakes for $.25 and delicious pies for $.20. Al and Louis, in October of 1962, made some comments about these prices saying that nowadays they must pay the huge price of $.69 for the pies and cakes that were smaller and not as tasty. They would be truly shocked at the prices of the present day. Louis quoted some prices from an old log book: 1 peck of potatoes, 2 dozen eggs, and 1 dozen bananas, $1.05. On one trip up the canal (4-5 days) May, 1913, the food bill for the three man crew was $5.05.

By the time they pulled the three miles to Patterson's store below the lock at Moses Kill, it was midnight so they tied up for the night. It was a not muggy night and mosquitoes were out in great numbers. The store was open and Mr. Patterson was there. A call was made to Gus Regner at Fort Edward and arrangements made for him to come down with his nice team of horses and take them in tow.

The next morning, July 3, they locked through Moses Kill Lock and pulled by hand until they met Gus Regner and his team near Satterlee's on the five mile level above Moses Kill. He hooked onto the boat and, because of its shallow draft, easily moved it along. Tugboat men, towing northbound coal boats, considered themselves lucky to complete this hard towing five mile level in eight hours. It usually took more. The team pulled them through Fort Edward and through the Brewery Lock onto the twelve mile Summit level. It was another very hot day with temperatures over ninety degrees so they pulled up to the waste weir five miles south of Fort Ann to have dinner and to feed and rest the horses. When preparing to get underway again Louis looked back and saw a man walking up the tow path. He thought it looked like his father so they delayed their departure and sure enough it was Captain Vandervoort, owner and captain of the *Annex*, who had left Whitehall on the D & H Railroad to come meet them. He had watched through the train window and after seeing them, got off at Fort Edward where he hired a team to overtake them. It was so hot that the hired team gave out and he continued on foot. It was fortunate that the tow had not started sooner and thus made it much more difficult for him to catch them. The horse team now continued on with the boat and covered the five miles to Fort Ann which completed the contract with Gus Regner. The stipulated fee had been five dollars but they were so pleased with the service that they paid six.

The father wanted to tie up above the lock and rest up but the others wanted to be on their way so they started locking down through the double locks. Their brother Will Vandervoort met them there. He had walked the twelve miles from Whitehall on that hot day to meet them and help with the tow. Now the three brothers acted as the team doing the towing and the father acted as steerman with a big oar over the stern. They pulled over the one quarter mile level, locked down in the single lock, and continued on to Wood Lock where they tied up for the night.

Next morning, July 4, the wind had shifted to the north and it became very cold. The three young men were unable to pull the houseboat against the wind. The Line tug *Whitehall* came along with a tow of canal boats and added the houseboat to the tow. Al was clad only in his underwear but he got on the tow to take the lines from the houseboat to the last boat. This last canal boat was light and very high so they were not able to hold the family floating home up close to it. The distance between them was so great that Al was unable to get back to his own boat. Being ill dressed for the cold weather, he shivered while the two miles was covered to the Guard Lock where he was able to change to the other boat and warm clothes.

On arrival at Whitehall five miles later, the boat was locked down through the triple locks into Lake Champlain. The *Annex* took them in tow and had hard towing the 25 miles down the lake against the wind. They tied up that night at the boom at Ticonderoga and after such very hot days it became so cold that night that it made a little ice in the water pails. Louis remembers that as July 4, 1910, the night of the Johnson- Jefferies fight which Jefferies lost.

Chapter 8

The Canaler and His Boat

The successful canalboat owner and operator was a good business man. He had to have the ability to contract for a load that paid well and would not damage his boat beyond the usual wear and tear. A good contract called for a destination where a return load could be picked up. Carrying cargo in each direction was desirable. Running the boat empty was a red ink proposition.

In the spring of the year, he wanted to load and get to Waterford as soon as possible, even though the canal might not be opened for several weeks. With hundreds of boats at Waterford, Lansingburg, Cohoes, and Troy, waiting for the opening day, the early birds avoided a big delay. Time was money. An extra trip might mean the difference between a normal season and a great one. Canalers wanted to keep moving and hated the time lost to rest a team or, in the case of a tug, to rest a crew. On arrival at Waterford, perhaps a month or more early, he would stock up on groceries, rope, kerosene, and other necessities. A store like Nealer's would carry him on the books and charge interest of about six per cent. Hard cash was needed to pay expenses on the trip so the boatman, if running short, might take out a loan to carry him until he collected for his first load.

The boatman, besides having the brains to handle financial matters had to have the brawn to handle the hard work in the canal and to stand up to the occasional bully he might meet. He had to know the canal and its way of operation. Maintaining his vessel was very important so he had to know how to locate leaks and to stop them. A basic knowledge of carpentry, caulking, and painting, allowed him to make minor repairs and thus avoid the expense and lost time of stopping at a boatyard. Most boatmen took good care of their vessels. One could see them in the morning bailing water from the canal with a bucket on a lanyard and washing down the deck. Many owners took great pride in their vessels. When in my early years, I noticed that many of the privately owned barges were painted white. I asked a boatman about it and was told that he did not like to buy prepared paint. he preferred to mix white lead with linseed oil to make his own. Black was added if he wanted a shade of gray.

The canal boats of that day varied greatly in the amount of comfort and good living conditions available to the inhabitants. The young man just starting out would have a mortgaged, leaking, vessel with a small cabin very scantly furnished. A family man would have a boat built with more comfortable quarters. The cabin could have as many as four small rooms but this was not the usual. Some had a large room which could be divided off by curtains. The size of the cabin could be seen by what projected above the deck but inside the lower part of the cabin extended to the sides and stern of the boat. When a bunk was built into this space it was called a cuddy. Drawers and closets were built under the beds and in the other spaces. Sometimes the table would be hinged to a bulkhead so it could be folded down when not in use thus allowing more living room. Occasionally, a couple of bunks would be installed in the storage space under to the bow deck. This would be used by older boys in a large family or, if the family was small or young, by a steersman. under the stern deck was a small storage space called the "Booby hatch." young children were threatened with being put in the booby hatch if they misbehaved.

Two windows on each side of the cabin was the usual rule. Entrance to the cabin was by way of a small door usually on the left side of the after wall of the house. A hatch cut into the roof at this point and fitted with a sliding hatch cover allowed people to enter the cabin down a short series of steps. Windows were often fitted with sliding wooden shutters which recessed into the wall when not in use. These shutters protected the glass windows, protected the people from prying eyes, and provided a means of ventilation and protection from the water during a rainstorm. Water for drinking and cooking was carried in a wooden barrel. Water from Lake Champlain north of Split Rock was considered

Waiting for opening of canal at Waterford.
Photo, NYS Archives.

John Savage and Elvia, Fort Edward 1905
Photo, Frank Godfrey.

**When canal boats collected in one place the women
visited each other and the men held bull sessions.**
Photo, Frank Godfrey

Author's mother with "Weeping Willow".
Photo, Fred Godfrey

the best for drinking. In an emergency they might fill the water barrel from the Hudson River at Esopus Island. History says that this water was preferred by the old Hudson River whaling ships because it kept longer in the barrel. The canal, lake, or river, provided all water for other uses. Heat for cooking and comfort came from the use of coal or wood. Kerosene lamps and lanterns were in use for light. This may sound very crude and unappealing but it was not such a bad way of life. The men and boys worked very hard in the canal but on lakes and rivers it was different. An awning frame above the cabin on which a canvas tarp was stretched kept the cabin cooler. This provided a place to sling a hammock for sleeping and a place for a rocking chair in which to rest, read, knit, or gossip with the neighbors when in a big tow. It also became a playground for the toddler in the family who was hitched into a leather harness and connected to a rope which allowed him the run of the cabin roof but prevented him from getting off. Depending on the family, the cabin could be a snug, homey, comfortable place of refuge from the cold and wet. In winter, the boatman could layover in his own hometown or anywhere new that he wanted to try, and pay no taxes. Most spent the winters in New York Harbor at one of the many places where the canalers congregated. This was when the children were sent to school. Whole communities of boatmen and their families existed there and soon everyone knew the neighbors. They also went sightseeing, repaired their boats, and held parties and bull sessions. I remember a saying I once heard about the canal boat owner in New York in winter. It was said that even though he had not worked since last fall there was no time that the canaler could not pull a twenty dollar bill out of his pocket.

I have heard many old timers extol the benefits and pleasures of canal boat life and their sorrow at seeing it come to an end. It had its good points and its drawbacks but was not a bad way of life.

The stories which follow were sent to me by my cousin Madeline Marks and were taken from the collection of her father, Captain Frank H. Godfrey. They illustrate one type of man who was a Champlain Canal boatman an also illustrates one of the dangers of canaling.

Prior to 1880 or 1890 all boats on the Northern (Champlain) Canal were single units. The crew consisted of the captain, who in most cases was the owner, his mate or deckhand, and if married, his wife and children.

Among the several owner-captains from the village of Fort Edward was George Ellis who owned and operated the canal boat *Egger Hill*. Ellis always had a slight grin on his face so that it was impossible to know if he were glad or angry. He spoke with a slow drawl and was never known to become excited. Though he walked about the deck of his boat in such a slow, awkward manner as to lead a person to believe he was the most clumsy man on the entire canal, if the occasion arose, he could be as quick and nimble as a cat.

While discharging a cargo of coal at Fort Edward one summer day his mate quit. He then hired a young man from a farm near Argyle who desired to leave farm life for, as he thought, a life of thrills and excitement on the canal. When the unloading was completed Captain Ellis proceeded north by canal to Whitehall. here he placed his boat in the tow of the tug *Glen Iris* which was leaving for Burlington, Vt. with a tow of canal boats.

The following morning the boat dropped off from the tow at Port Henry where it was to be loaded with iron ore for New York City. Due to a light westerly off-shore summer breeze the boat, being light, lost its headway while still a considerable distance form the shore. As was customary when "dropping off" from a tow on Lake champlain, Ellis had his anchor stocked and ready on the port side deck. An anchor warp was attached to the anchor with a few coils of the line coiled near, and forward of, the anchor so as to avoid fouling when the anchor was dropped. The warp then went through the port bow chock with a couple of turns around the port bow bitt.

When the boat lost its steerage way Ellis left the tiller, ran to the anchor, and up-ended it over the side. In doing so he accidentally stepped into one of the coils of the anchor warp and was pulled over the side ant taken to the bottom with the anchor. Fortunately the water at that point was only fifteen to eighteen feet deep. On reaching the bottom he managed to free his foot from the anchor warp before the boat settled back onto the warp

88

as otherwise he might have drowned. When he reached the surface of the water he swam to the bow of the boat, climbed up the bow guards, paid out a little more on the anchor warp for a lead, and made it fast as though nothing had happened. He then turned to the farm lad who stood with mouth open, unable to move, and said with his slow drawl; "Well, I guess that will hold all right. I set it good. You know that is your job, but since you are green, I thought I would set it this time to show you how it is done." He then went aft to the cabin to change his clothes.

The wind died out shortly after sundown and they hoisted the anchor. Using the long setting poles which were always carried on the Champlain Canal boats, they poled the boat to the dock. As soon as they were close enough the farm lad jumped to the dock and, without waiting for his clothes or pay, shouted to Captain Ellis; "I quit. I'll be damned if I am going to set anchors on the bottom of the lake for you or anyone else." he then took off down the dirt road on his long walk to Fort Edward.

On June 9, 1884 the *Anna Hathaway* was bound south in the canal with a hundred and sixty-eight thousand feet of white pine lumber for a cargo, the deckload of which barely cleared the canal bridges. The captain and owner of the boat, not yet twenty-five years old, with his wife a year younger, had worked hard and saved every penny possible to have this boat built. Late in the fall of 1883 he had signed a contract with Louis Stone, a Whitehall boat builder, with a boatyard in the village, to build this boat during the winter. Shortly after the canal opened, the following spring, the boat was launched.

As his first cargo he took aboard a full load of hard coal at the Elbow coal docks at Whitehall bound for Chambly, Canada. After discharging this coal at Chambly he proceeded light to Hull, Ontario where he loaded a cargo of white pine lumber for New York City. No delays for tows, nor weather, were encountered on the trip south. On June 9, 1884 he found there was "high water at the river" (at Northumberland) but he succeeded in crossing without any delay. Arriving at Schuylerville, the Line team was replaced by a fresh one at the Line barn. Darkness was approaching so the mate lighted the bow lamp and then retired to his bunk in the bow of the boat.

89

It was a warm, clear, June night and the captain was on the high raised steering platform steering with a false tiller which enabled him to see over the high deck load of lumber. The bow lamp allowed his some visibility ahead of the boat. He could see the driver and the team and at times see a spark as the iron shoe of a mule struck a stone on the towpath. By midnight, when he would call his mate, they would be out of the short bends and in better going for the rest of the night. It did not look as if there would be any fog so he would be able to get a few hours of good sleep before breakfast was ready at six in the morning. The young boat owner was well pleased with the success he was enjoying with his new boat.

He speculated that, with a good run this night, they might make tomorrow night's tow out of Albany for New York. There, after unloading the lumber, he could load sugar for Montreal, then go light from Montreal to Ottawa, and return to New York with another load of lumber. He could then load coal at one of the coal ports for Fort Edward or Whitehall and then look for a load of potatoes to take to New York for the winter. This would bring in enough money to finish paying what he still owed on the boat. He dreamed contentedly on. "Not bad. Not bad at all. A new prime built boat of the canal all paid for. A three thousand dollar boat, free and clear, at my age. At this rate I will soon have a home ashore where we can spend our winters." His dreams were interrupted before he called his mate that night.

On the sixteen mile level, about five miles south of Schuylerville and one mile south of Coveville, on the towpath side of the canal, stood Costello's grocery and day-boat barn. Another half mile to the south from the grocery was his home. Between the grocery and his home a cove extended from the Hudson River to the outside bank of the canal towpath. This cove, with a depth of about ten feet, was something like thirty-five feet or more below the canal level.

At 11:15 p.m. the *Anna Hathaway* passed Costello's grocery. When about midway between the grocery and the house, the towpath between the team and the boat slid into the cove without any warning. The driver snapped the towline free of the team and ran them farther along the towpath so they would not be carried away with the rapidly disappearing bank. The *Hathaway* was carried by the force of the water, bow first, through the break, into the cove, and then into the river, followed by sixteen miles of water from the canal. The boatman sprang from his steering platform to the stern deck and down the stairway into the cabin to get his wife and found her sleeping peacefully. He then climbed onto the deckload and ran forward and jumped down into the mate's sleeping quarters expecting to find him hurt but he also was asleep. Until called, neither the wife nor the mate knew that the boat had taken the drop from the canal into the river. On examination, it was found that the boat had sustained no damage and not one board was missing nor disturbed from the deckload. The force of the water had carried the boat into the river without allowing it to contact the bank of the canal. The break carried away between eight and nine hundred feet of the towpath and canal bottom. it took a great number of men and teams nearly a month to repair, and cost the state over fourteen thousand dollars.

After the break had been repaired the lumber was unloaded from *Anna Hathaway* onto wagons, and teams drew it back to the canal where it was again loaded onto a boat for New York. The *Hathaway* was then floated down the Hudson another two miles to the Willow grocery where she was put on weighs and, with blocks and tackles leading to Spanish windlasses which were operated by teams of horses, she was hauled back onto the towpath and then into the canal.

The young skipper had his boat ready to operate just in time to load potatoes in the fall. He had lost a season's work plus one hundred dollars deductible.

Looking South From Lock 10   Northumberland

Chapter 9

Changes

W ith the opening of the Champlain Barge Canal came many changes. The old canal was closed except for a section from the Five Combines through Lock 15 at Fort Edward to the new Junction Lock which connected the Feeder to the new and larger canal. South of this junction lock, the canal bank had washed out and this, plus the new digging, had caused a wide water to be formed in the new canal. This is known locally as Kinser's Lake, named after an ice dealer who cut his ice there. The Glens Falls Feeder now supplied the water to the summit level of the new canal between Locks #8 and #9.

The more modern canal meant the end of towing by horses and mules. Drivers and steersmen were no longer needed. The Line barns and the resting sheds and barns along the canal were closed. Saloons on or near the locks lost their business and none were allowed on the new locks. Small businesses like grocery stores, suffered as did some larger ones which had used the old waterway as a means of transportation.

Photos opposite page:
1913 - After the washout.
Photo, Jim Petit
1913 - Washout at Lock #10, Northumberland.
Photo, Jim Petit
What happens with a break in the canal bank.
Photo, Frank Godfrey

Bigger tugs were coming in to compete for the towing but in a few years these so called bigger tugs would be considered very small. The little *Annex* was still towing and she had one advantage over the other towboats. Being only 42 ft. long, she could lock crosswise in the locks. The Glens Falls Feeder boats, being narrow, could lock three abreast in the new locks, thus the *Annex* could lock with nine of these boats in one locking. This never happened because there would never be nine Feeder boats together at one time. Other northern boats could lock two abreast so the little tug could lock crosswise ahead of six of them. This tug, with tows of this size, would be a single locking while larger tugs would have to make a double locking with consequent loss of time. The size of the old locks had restricted the size of the canal boats but now they were being built larger and called barges. These larger boats were able to carry more cargo but they never came near to the capacity of the big "boxes" which appeared at a later day.

Most barge captains took good care of their vessels. One could see them in the morning bailing water from the river with a pail on a lanyard and washing down the deck. Minor repairs, caulking above the water line, and painting, were all handled by the barge captain-owner. Hardwood fenders were now hung along the sides of the boats. This had not been possible in the old canal because of the narrow locks which the boats could barely squeeze into.

The normal tow for a tug in the old canal, was four boats. This was the tug with a single towline or hawser to the first pair of boats which were coupled together one behind the other so they could be steered. A towline, of about 150 ft. ran from the stern of the second boat to the bow of the third boat which was coupled to the fourth boat so they could be steered. The tug might tow as many as ten boats in this fashion if they were lightly loaded and traveling south with the current. The large tows caused congestion and loss of time at the locks so, sometime after the opening of the Barge Canal, the State decreed that tows would be restricted to a double locking. This edict is still in effect but, with no tows operating, there is no need to enforce it.

Towing four barges with an intermediate hawser between the first and second pair did not last long once the Champlain

Proposed location for Junction Lock at Fort Edward, April 28, 1905

Building the Junction Lock at Fort Edward, April 28, 1908.
This and above Photo, NYS Archives

Junction Lock, Ft. Edward after feeder canal abandoned.
Photo, Canal Society of NYS

Dredge, "Fort Edward" Working in Barge Canal, Fort Ann, N.Y.

Barge Canal was fully open. Boats were bunched up one behind the other and the only steering done was between the first and second boats. A canal boat had a moulded or rounded bow so that when being steered behind another boat, there was no bow corner to interfere with putting a kink in the tow. With the advent of the square bowed "boxes" their square corners created a problem becaue the corner would contact the boat ahead and the tow could not be steered. The solution to this problem was the "bustle bumper." The bustle on a canal boat was the section projecting outward across the top of the stern which supported the rudder post. The bumper was a large timber hung vertically from the middle of the bow of the second boat which kept the two vessels separated so that they could be steered without the corner hitting the boat ahead. This same system was used later on the Erie Barge Canal on the large boxes such as those of the Hedger Transportation Company. The wheelsman could not steer these big barges but he could assist the tug in turning them. Iron ore from Port Henry was carried on large, square-cornered deckscows on the Champlain Barge Canal. There were no steering wheels on these scows so they were coupled togehter rather loosely and the tug was thus able to turn them.

The boatman had to work hard when towing in the old Champlain Canal. The hours were long and sleeping time was short and unpredictable. Work involved at locks, or when wedged, or when using block lines, was strenuous. When underway, each single boat and each double header required a steers man. The new and larger canal caused a great change in the amount of work required of a bargeman. In my day on the

Photos opposite page:
**Hudson Valley Railway piers south of
Fort Edward and formation of Kinser's Lake.**
Photo, NYS Archives
Dredge *Fort Edward* working on Barge Canal at Fort Ann.
Photo, NYS Archives
New locks have larger capacity.
Lock 4 canal boats and tug instead of just one boat.
Photo, Jim Petit

97

Northern Canal, we put a hawser on each bow corner of the head boat and no bargeman steered a tow regardless of what type of boat or how equipped. His only work, when transitting the canal, was putting out a snubbing line at each lock.

The canal boats had carried many different cargoes but the strangest was live eels. Bill Cleary said they were shipped in canal boats. In the fall, the boat was pumped half full of water in Canada and live eels put in. The boat was towed to Fulton Fish Market in New York, the eels removed, and the boat pumped out. He said the eels were in demand by Greek and Italian people in the city. Nothing was said about any residual odors in the canal boat.

I never knew of the eels shipped in barges but in my day there were two eel boats that were towed to New York in the fall and towed back to Canada in the spring. They were frail craft, merely pontoons supporting a fine mesh cage which allowed water to flow through. The last one I saw was in 1936 when, as mate on the *Madeline Murray*, we towed one back to Canada on the first trip of the year.

The locks had changed from the small wooden structures to locks of cut stone and then to the larger and fewer locks of reinforced concrete. The hard physical labor required to operated the old locks was replaced by electricity to operate the gates, valves, winches, etc. No longer were the men called lock keepers or locktenders. Now they are called operators and the job is not restricted to males.

Now to "fast forward" through more recent Champlain Canal history—with the opening of the barge canal in 1915 the canal boats could be built bigger. They were still restricted in length, width, and depth, to the size of the locks in the Canadian Chambly Canal if they ran in or out of Canada, but they still carried more cargo. The good years were soon over as the competition of the D & H Railroad, motor trucks, and other factors cut down the volume of freight. The days of large daily tows on Lake Champlain came to an end and in something over ten years The Line ceased to exist. Canal boat owners sold their barges. Some went ashore to live while others ran barges for wages. I believe that by 1933 when I started work there were less

Nellie Ralph Capt. Herman Dayton owner,
Chas. Paquette at wheel.
Photo, NYS Archives

An ugly tug owned by The Line.
Photo, Jim Petit

than ten independent boat owners on the Champlain Canal. Murray Transortation Company, with offices in New York City and a field office in North Troy, owned all the other barges and carried all the dry cargo through this waterway. Many former boat owners now worked for them. another company owned by the same people and frequently called Murray's, was the Lake Champlain Despatch Company. This company controlled the towing on this canal and was the only one towing into St. Jean, P.Q., Canada. it operated a fleet of old tugs some of which had been owned by The Line.

The brief period of prosperity enjoyed by Murray ended when less freight became available. Their best paying freight had been rolls of newsprint paper from Gatineau in Canada to pier 6 in New York City. The Canadian paper companies built self-propelled, steel, vessels the size of the Chambly Canal locks to do this work. When there were enough of them built to carry all of the paper, Murray lost its best source of income. They carried the same tonnage as a canal barge but made a trip much faster and operated at less expense. Our wages at that time of depression were not great but the paper boat crews were paid about half as much.

The first Canadian paper boats to come down, the *News Carrier*, hired U.S. pilots for the first one or two trips. As the second vessel was built, the mate on the first one became master of the second one, and he taught his new mate the route. Thus as each new little freighter was built the mate moved to master and broke in a new mate. These tin cans were soon setting records for poor navigation and poor ship handling. Many stories were told of their mis-adventures. Despite their shallow 6' 6" draft I have seen them aground in Lake Champlain and the Hudson River. I know of one running into the head boat of an iron ore tow on the lake. When I was mate on the *Madeline Murray*, tied up below Lock #3, one left the lock and ran right into me. Luckily it was a glancing blow and neither ship was in jured. The canal was once tied up for a week when one of these craft ran into the lower gate at Lock #11 and put it out of operation. It seemed to me that banging into things was not considered unusual by the crews. One day, when on the *Billy Murray* tied up in St. Jean, a Canadian

100

paper boat came down the Richelieu River and approached the dock to tie up. The pilot ran smack into the concrete wall putting a dent in his port bow quarter. Immediately after the mooring lines were out the deckhand jumped on the dock with a can of paint and a brush and painted over the scraped mark on the hull. It looked as though a can of paint was kept handy to cover up scars caused by poor ship handling. Despite the fresh paint, the dent was very visible.

Canal boats towing through the Chambly Canal with tractors, or previously with animals, had always been required by the Candian government to carry a steersman. I was told that he was usually a very old man or a teen-ager who, more often than not, merely rode through the canal and did nothing for his pay.

Some of the unemployed U.S. tugboat pilots tried to get the job of piloting the Canadians through U.S. waters but were refused. They appealed to their union and the longshoremen refused to unload the paper at Pier 6 until pilots were hired. Well, that caused a furor and the confetti hit the fan. Representatives of the U.S. State Department were soon on hand, calling the strike illegal as a U.S. - Canadian treaty allowed free use of each others waterways. The strike was over and nothing was accomplished.

Murray's tugs and barges decreased in number and finally disappeared during WW II. The Candians lasted quite a bit longer but they are also gone. The movement of petroleum products to Lake Champlain ports kept the canal in use in the years after WW II but has now decreased to almost nothing. Now in the middle of the 1993 season there has been just one tug operating in the canal pushing an oil barge.

In this chapter about changes, I must mention the change in the going-ashore clothes. Louis Vandervoort said that when he was a deckhand and got a night off in Waterford he would go to Rensselaer Park or Murtle Beach Park, get a dollars worth of nickles, and have a great time. He dressed for the occasion in red flannel underwear with long sleeves. Over this he wore a blue flannel shirt with the sleeves rolled up to display the red flannel underneath. This in summer weather! That was considered real sporty attire.

Changes also occurred to Lake Champlain. This beautiful body of water is no longer a commercial waterway and the era of the big excursion steamers is long gone. Today it is extensively used by pleasure boaters. Recent efforts to attract tourists have publicized the existence of "Champ," a large unidentified creature, with several sightings reported. In all my years of conversation with people who spent time on Lake Champlain such as family members, old time tugboat and canal boat people, captains of passenger vessels and ferry boats, hunters, fishermen, and yachtsmen, I never heard any mention of such a mammal. Photographs have been taken of something in the lake which lends some credence to the story of "Champ," but I am not convinced.

There was one story that made the rounds of Murray's tugboat men that relates to such a creature. In the early 1930s the tug *Defender*, Clayton H. Godfrey master, came off the lake into Whitehall with a tow from Canada. The canal was open only sixteen hours per day that year so the tug, having only a single crew, went through the lock with the tow and tied up at the canal terminal. The old bow fenders had been removed from the tug and the sharp steel bow had been chipped to remove rust, wire brushed, and coated with red lead in preparation for painting and hanging new fenders. Feeling the need for some relaxation, the captain and the chief engineer went ashore for a few beers. They entered a bar where they met a man who acted as a part-time news gatherer for *The Whitehall Times*, a weekly newspaper. He had ovbiously been there for some time and he struck up a conversation with the two tugboat men.

"What's that red stuff all over the bow of your tug?" he wanted to know.

"Well," drawled the captain in reply, "that's blood from a big sea serpent we ran into on the lake."

The next issue of the weekly carried an item about a tug hitting a sea monster on the lake. I wonder how many people believed it.

**Last office of The Line at Whitehall,
as it looked June 20, 1993.**
Photo, Fred Godfrey

Tug *Wm. H. Nealer.*   *Photo, Fred Godfrey*

Louis Vandervoort and tug *Comstock* behind oil barge *Seaboard #99* at Mechanicville Terminal, Oct. 1, 1941. Just looking to see what it was like to push a big barge.   *Photo, Fred Godfrey*

Early photo of *Comstock.* *Photo, Canal Society of NYS*

Chapter 10

Louis Vandervoort

L ouis Vandervoort witnessed the days of the mule skinners on the old canal, the competition of the little tugboats, the opening of the Barge Canal, and the bigger tugs with bigger barges. He started as a deckhand on the *Annex* for his father, served his apprenticeship,and became captain on several other tugs. From his talk, I suspect that the *Annex*, the *Marion*, and the *Comstock* were three of his favorites.

The *Annex* was remembered as the ship which he started sailing in as a boy, and as the pioneer of tugboat towing in the Champlain Canal. The Vandervoort family had fond memories of the *Annex*.

The tug *Marion* was one that Louis enjoyed working on. Jake Holler's Construction Co. of Fort Edward was engaged in dredging and other work preparing for the opening of the Champlain Barge Canal. He bought the steam yacht *Marion* on Lake George and his foreman, a very able man named Jim Doyle, brought her right down the streets of Ticonderoga and floated her in Lake Champlain. The ship was 62 ft. long, 10-12 ft. wide, and 4-5 ft. deep. It was powered by a pipe boiler feeding steam to a fore and aft compound condensing engine. That is a two cylinder, two crank engine which does not exhaust the spent steam directly into the air. She was converted to a tug and Louis Vandervoort went aboard as captain. Having been a yacht, her accommodations were palatial compared to the ordinary tug. The added room allowed the captain to bring his wife aboard for extended periods of time. She sometimes brought a young girl with her named Edie Taylor. One time, when engaged in towing mud scows and dumping them in the bends of Wood Creek, they were halted by a farmer on shore with a loaded shotgun. He pointed the gun toward the tug and warned them not to dump there in front of his farm. Louis decided that the shotgun was a persuasive argument in the farmer's favor so he dumped the scow elsewhere.

The *Comstock* was a fine looking, well kept, handy little tug, built at Croton-on-Hudson in 1911, and named *Charles H. Pike*. When she came up the Champlain Canal to begin towing, she was considered a big tug. Not many years after the opening of the Champlain Barge Canal, she was considered rather small. At one point she was purchased by The Line and renamed *Comstock* as it was their custom to name tugs after places on the Champlain Canal. The Vandervoort family purchased her to replace the *Annex* which was cut in half by the *Albany Socony* at Mechanicville in 1921.

When I started work as a deckhand in the summer of 1933, the *Comstock* was working for the State of New York assisting tows in and out of Lock #3. The crew was Louis Vandervoort as captain, his brother Al Vandervoort as engineer, and Billy Gandreau was deckhand. It was said that the Vandervoort tugs got this job because of a favor Louis' father had done the state years ago by helping to remove a bridge which had fallen across the canal at Wilbur's Basin. It was the longest span over the canal and it fell down with a herd of cows crossing on it right in front of the tug and tow, effectively blocking the canal. Canal Superintendent, Will Hickey of Mechanicville (who lived to be over 100 years old), came up with some workmen to remove the bridge. A long towline and a snatchblock to a deadman on a side hill as used to pull sections of the bridge out piece by piece. The tug was used for the power needed and the towline was damaged but no bill was submitted to the state even though one was requested. The captain was more interested in getting under way. No compensation was received then but it paid off later.

Superintendent Hickey also admired the work done by Louis. When the new canal was opened, it was found that the contractor, who did the dredging below Lock #5 at Schuylerville, had removed the gravel but left rocks in the channel. The *Charles H. Pike* (later the *Comstock*) came up the river with a tow and struck the rocks and could find no deep channel to Lock #5. The river soon had a couple of hundred boats jammed up waiting to go north. Great Lakes Dredge and Dock Company came in with drill boats to dynamite the rocks. They worked there all summer and a channel was marked out with one gallon syrup cans, plain on the west side, with bottoms painted red on the east side. It seems natural that they called it the tin can channel. Louis was on the *William H. Nealer*, a tug of rather shallow draft. He was given the job of towing boats up through this channel, at first one at a time, then two, then more, and as things improved the tows went on.

These events may have influenced the decision when a tug was desired at Mechanicville. New York State hired the *Annex* to assist tows in and out of the lower end of Lock #3. Below this lock, the water from the papermill rushed across the river and through the piers on the east side. These piers were faced with a heavy wooden boom which boats could slide along but must be pulled off of before reaching the lower end where there was hard rock. Because of the action of these currents, the tows would snake into an S configuration and had to be straightened out to go through the narrow draw of the bridge that was there at that time. The *Comstock*, which replaced the sunken *Annex* in 1921, worked on the tail end of the tow helping to keep things in shape. In the 1930s, when the Lake Champlain Company's steamboats were bringing down four 1,000 ton scows heavily loaded with iron ore from Port Henry, the *Comstock* was always there to help. This was a difficult spot for the pilots to navigate safely.

One summer night in 1936, about 2 a.m., I came down to Lock #3 with four iron ore scows. I was mate on the *Madeline Murray*, a twenty year old, newly licensed pilot. The tug and first two scows had locked down and were waiting below the lock for the other two when the *Comstock* came alongside. "Is that you Buster?" (my nickname) asked Captain Vandervoort. When I replied in the affirmative he asked, "Are you taking the tow down?" Again I said yes and Louis shook his head in disbelief but said no more. He probably visualized some, or all, of the tow sunk or wrapped around a bridge abutment. I wasn't too confident myself and Louis' apparent doubt didn't help. Because of my training, I had no difficulty, but was relieved when the tug and tow was safely through the bridge. I'm sure Louis was relieved also.

The *Comstock* was also supposed to assist tows against the current up to the lock. I don't know what was needed in earlier days but it was not needed in my time. The crew of the little tug was very well liked so no one objected when she put a line on the tow and pulled along up to the lock. Without this appearance of helping the tows, the state might have canceled their contract.

Captain "Mike" Lafountain, on the tug *Defender*, came up the river one day pushing an oil barge along at a pretty good speed. He kept her "hooked up" and the *Comstock* was unable to put a towline on the barge. Crew members of the large tug sent friendly hoots of derision toward the crew of the smaller tug as she pulled away. This was not done maliciously but as a practical joke.

As an illustration of how the captains and mates on Murray's Lake Champlain Despatch Company tugs felt about the little tug and her crew, I submit the following. It was rumored that the state was going to replace the *Comstock* with their steam tug *Urger*. On hearing this, Murray's pilothouse men got word to the state that they would not permit the *Urger* to touch their tows as the experience of Capt. Vandervoort and the maneuverability of the *Comstock* could not be matched by the *Urger* and her crew. The change was never made. I know not how much she was needed in earlier days of small tugs and canal boat tows but in my day, we could get along with her help. A few years later, as the canal traffic in hawser tows diminished, she was released by the state. I always admired the little ship and I feel that she was the favorite of favorites for Louis.

Winters, he acted as manager of the family business, Dunne's Paint Store in Waterford. We boatmen, who might be home, often met in the backroom of this store. We called it "The Spit and Whittle Club." Louis always presided at these sessions dressed in his usual uniform of blue serge trousers, starched white shirt with necktie, dark blue coat sweater, and grey cap. Discussions were held about all phases of tugboat life. The participants in the backroom meeting would do more boating in one hour than could be accomplished in a week on the canal. Many were the stories they told, but very few about the old Champlain Canal. I regret that I never questioned Louis, nor my parents, nor my grandparents about that period in our history.

My last contact with the *Comstock* occurred October 1, 1941. I was working for James McWilliams Blue Line of New York City and was given the job of taking a loaded oil barge (*Seaboard* #99) to Mechanicville. It contained fuel oil for the papermill and was pumped out at the pier below Lock #3. When empty, the barge was turned around and landed at the terminal to take on water ballast. This was not done at the pier where the cargo was discharged because the depth of the barge in ballast would make it very difficult, if not impossible, to turn around in the narrow channel. When the barge was ballasted, I persuaded Louis to put the *Comstock* behind the barge and see what he thought of pushing an oil barge. The *Comstock* looked rather small in the notch in the stern of the tanker. Captain Vandervoort opined that he did not want any of those pushing jobs.

Louis Vandervoort spent his working years on tugboats as I did and our experiences in some ways are similar. We both spent our early years working hard on tugs with very little conveniences for the crew. Conditions improved for each of us. He spent his later years on a job of very little work and was home every night and I worked a week on board ship and a week home. The similarity ends there.

He worked on single crew tugs which tied up every night (sometimes for only a short time) and I worked on double crew tugs that ran twenty-four hours a day. His normal range of work was the sixty miles between Waterford and Whitehall, while a generation later the pilots were expected to work lakes, bays, sound, rivers, and coastwide, all over the northeast, and also on the Great Lakes. The tugs featured in this book were low powered, coal burning, steam boats, with no crew comforts while today there are no steam tugs and the diesels are vessels of high horsepower, pilot house control, equipped with radio, radar, refrigeration, comfortable quarters, air conditioning, and TV. What a change!

It is not my purpose to denigrate the pilots on those early canal tugboats but rather to show the changes that occurred in one generation with the closing of the Champlain Canal and the opening of the Champlain Barge Canal. One whole way of life and mode of transportation died and the mode that replaced it is almost gone.

Comstock when owned and operated by The Line.
Photo, Jim Petit

Oct. 1, 1941, Mechanicville Terminal.
Photo, Fred Godfrey

Chapter 11

A Canal Family

Many families can trace their roots back to an ancestor who got his start running a canalboat. Some take pride in it, some do not acknowledge it, and some do not even know it. When I was younger, I often had elderly men approach me and tell me with great delight of their early years and their experiences on canalboats. One man, a machine shop owner, was a member of a canalboat family. In his youth he had met another boy of the same age and they had palled around together working on boats and picking fruit in the Hudson Valley. He told me the other boy was named Charlie Beckett. imagine our surprise when we found that this was the same Charlie Beckett who was finishing out his career as my deckhand on a tug in New York Harbor. I am at least a fourth generation member of a canalboat family. My great-grandfather, Henry Walrod, operated a boat in the old canal. His daughter, my grandmother, Alice Etta Walrod, who lived in Fort Edward, occasionally rode with him as cook. Granddad went ashore and he sold the boat to his son Frank, who did quite well with it. He built it up into a fleet of four boats and operated so successfully that he was able to retire a few years after the Barge Canal opened.

My grandmother met and married my grandfather who was a printer on the newspaper *The Fort Edward Advertiser*. They had four sons, Frank, George, Clayton, and Fred, and when my grandfather's health failed and he could no longer work, a boat was purchased. The family went aboard and the boat was operated by my grandmother and the older boys. My grandfather died on this boat one night while returning from Canada, crossing Lake Champlain. As the three older boys became teen-agers, they went out on their own operating canalboats for a time before switching to tugboats. The fourth, or youngest, went directly to tugs and all four became tugboat captains.

My grandmother lived in Waterford for a few years in a big house right at the junction of the Mohawk and the Hudson River. Her friends from the canalboats would often come to visit and stay overnight or for a few days. Big as the house was, I sometimes slept on the floor on a feather tick because the beds were full. The stories told of experiences in Canada, New York, Buffalo, and points in between were fascinating to this young boy. I wish I could remember them now.

Following the family tradition, I spent some time on tugboats as a boy and went to work as a deckhand upon graduating from high school in 1933. I spent 40 years in the industry retiring at the end of 1973. The changes in that time span were just as great as those recorded in this book. Living conditions, wages, and tugboats, gradually improved and I can truthfully say that I worked during the best of the tugboat era. In my last years, I was aboard ship for one week and home for one week alternately throughout the year.

The fifth generation did not last long on boats. My son worked for me as deckhand for a short period but did not continue. It's just as well. Water transportation in this area is dead, the old steam tugs are history, and the canal is now just a yachtman's playground.

Sept. 1938. Spring floods were common and occasionally they occurred in the fall. This is Waterford Terminal looking east from Fourth St. bridge. Note the large "boxes" which came into use on the Barge Canal. *Photo, Fred Godfrey*

Glossary

Aqueduct - A structure for carrying the canal over a stream, river, road or hollow. The supporting piers were of stone and the section carrying water for the boats was of wood.

Ballast - Weight carried in the hold of a vessel to make it deeper in the water when without cargo.

Berm - The side of the canal opposite the towpath and called by boatmen the heelpath.

Bilge - The inside bottom of a boat where water collects from leakage.

Bitt - A vertical timber or metal casting, usually in pairs, for attaching hawsers or lines.

Booby Hatch - A small storage space in the stern of a canal boat.

Boxes - Large, square cornered barges used in the Barge Canal.

Bumboat - A boat carrying food, drink, newspapers, gloves, and other necessities for sale to the tows passing by.

Bustle - Built up section across stern of barge which supported the rudder post.

Bustle Bumper - A large timber hung vertically on bow of second boat in a double header to allow them to be steered.

Canal - An artificial waterway.

Canal Town - A settlement owing its existence and support to a canal.

Change Bridge - A bridge which allowed teams, when the towpath went from one side of the canal to the other, to cross over without having to disconnect the towline.

Clearance - Written permission from the state allowing the vessel to transit the canal to a certain point.

Cleat - A two ended piece of cast iron on the side deck of a vessel used to fasten a line to.

Cuddy - A small bunk space off the cabin of the canalboat.

Deadman - A post set in the ground as an anchor point used to pull against.

Double Header - Two canalboats coupled together one behind the other.

Dry Dock - A place where vessels may be floated in and the water removed so that work may be done on the vessel.

Eye Splice - A loop spliced in the end of a line.

Feeder Canal - A canal used to feed water to a canal system.

Guard Lock - A lock used to protect a canal from the danger of flooding by a nearby body of water.

Hames - Two wooden pieces that go around and project above a horses collar.

Hamming - Working for another deckhand who receives the pay while you receive only your meals and the experience.

Hawser - A large towline.

Head - The toilet facility on a vessel.

Heelpath - Opposite the towpath. The berm.

Hold - The section of a vessel where the cargo is carried.

Hooked Up - An expression used to indicate the engine is working at its full normal operating speed.

Horn of Cleat - Either end of the cleat.

Horse Bridge - A gangway used to get the towing animals on or off an Erie Canal boat.

Ice Boats - Boats used to transport ice to New York City before the days of refrigeration.

Lanyard - A section of rope about as large as ones finger, used for many purposes aboard ship.

Level - The level of water between two locks.

Light - A tug with no tow and a canalboat with no load.

Lighter - To remove all or part of the cargo from a boat.

Lock - A means of moving boats between two different levels of a canal.

Locktender - The man who operated the lock.

Miter Gate - One of a pair of gates used to seal off one end of a lock.

Miter Sill - The stone or concrete sill which the miter gates rest against when closed.

Mule Skinner - The driver of a mule team.

Paddles - A means of allowing water to flow into the upper end or out of the lower end of a lock. See wicket.

PSI - Pounds per square inch.

Running Light - A tug underway with no tow.
One of the red, white, or green, navigation lights.

Snatch Block - A block or pulley which can be opened on one side to receive the bight of a line.

Snub - To take headway off a vessel by rendering a rope around a post or cleat.

Snubbing Post - Vertical post used to snub on.

Spillway - A section of a dam over which excess water is allowed to flow.

Spring Pole - A sapling connected to the tin pump so as to assist in the operation of the pump on the up stroke.

Swelling - The opening of one or more wickets on the lower end of a lock to provide a swell of water along the level to assist a tow moving over it.

The Line - Logo of Lake Champlain Transportation Company.

Tiller - The arm on top of the rudder post which allowed the rudder to be turned.

Tiller Arm - The extension on the tiller which gave more leverage in operating the rudder and allowed the steersman to do this from the roof of the canalboat.

116

Tin Pump - A metal cylinder inserted in the pump box and running down to the bilge. It had a wood rod with a T handle which brought up water on its up stroke. The effort of raising this was eliminated by having a spring pole fastened to the handle which, after being pushed down, sprang back raising the water in the pump with no effort from the pumper.

Tow - One or more vessels being hauled along by team or tug.

Tow Cart - Two wheel cart used by driver who did not walk behind the animals.

Tow Line - Rope used to tow a vessel.

Tow Path - Side of canal on which the towing animals traveled.

Waste Weir - An overflow, or weir, for the escape of surplus water.

Water Ballast - Water used to sink a vessel deeper.

Wedged - Condition when tows attempting to pass get stuck because of the narrow channel.

Weeping Willow - See Spring Pole.

Weigh Lock - Place where boats were weighted to ascertain the tonnage carried.

Wicket - A small gate which can be opened to control the water level.

Wide Water - A section where the canal is wider than normal.

Index

Hudson Valley Railway, 24, 37
Huftil, Austin "Snub", 10

I

ice boats, 9
Inland Seaman's Store, 55
Inland Seaman's Union, 23, 52
International Paper Co., 65

J

Jackson, Stonewall, 64
Jake Holler's Construction
   Co., 105
James K. Averill, 63
James McWilliams Blue Line,
109
Jemson #1, 56
Junction Lock, 73, 93

K

Keenan Lime Co., 66
Kingston, NY, 33, 59, 80
Kinser's Lake, 93
knitting mill, 66

L

L. Thompson & Co., 7
La Chine Canal, 6
Lafountain, Mike, 108
Lake Champlain, 2, 32, 34, 51,
100, 102, 105
Lake Champlain Despatch Co.,
   (see Murray's L. C. Des. Co.)
Lake Champlain Trans. Co. , 6,
18, 23, 32, 37, 107
   (see The Line)
Lake George, 105
Lansingburg, NY, 83
Leddick, Bob, 24, 46
Leggett's Grocery Store, 23, 80
Lent, Abe "Dirty Dick", 37
Lester, Robert, 7
Lillian, 80
Lock #3, 101, 106 -107, 109
Lock #7, 65
Lock #8, 93
Lock #9, 93
Lock #11, 101

Lock #15, 28, 65, 93
   (see also Brewery Lock
   and Ft. Edward Lock)
Long Island Sound, 2
Lower River Lock, 27, 64, 80
Lower Two Lock, 17, 23, 79

M

Madeline Murray, 98, 101, 107
Mansfield, Hank, 80
Mansville's Drug Store, 52
Marion, 105
Marks, Madeline, 87
Marvel Shipyard, 34
Matton, Ralph, 56
Matton, Jesse, 55
Matton, John E., 55 -56, 79
McLaughlin, 79
McNaughton Towing Co., 6
Mechanicville, NY, 18, 40, 59,
106 -107
Millett's Saloon, 63
miter gate, 27, 31
Mohawk River, 112
moonshine, 79
Moses Kill, 24, 46, 81
Moses Kill Lock, 28, 64, 81
Moses Kill Creek, 28
Munson, John, 80
Murray Bay, 2
Murray Trans. Co., 56, 100
Murray's Lake Champlain
   Despatch Co., 56, 100, 108
Murray, Billy, 101
Murtle Beach Park, 102

N

Nealer's Store, 83
Nealer, William, 55
Ned Baker, 1
New York City, 2, 5, 9, 17, 59,
63, 66, 75, 87-88, 89, 90, 109
New York Harbor, 9, 66, 111
New York State Shops, 51
Newburgh, NY, 33 -34
News Carrier, 100
North River (Hudson River), 2

The Victors, 63
The Whitehall Times, 102
Thomas Gilchrist,64
Thomas Miller Jr., 10
Three Rivers, 2
Ticonderoga Creek, 34
Ticonderoga Pulp and
Paper Mill, 33 -34
Ticonderoga, NY, 79, 82, 105
trolleys, 24, 37
Troy, NY, 10, 37, 56, 83
tumble gate, 27, 55

U

Unique, 32
Upper River Lock, 27, 46, 64, 80
Upper Two Lock, 23, 28, 55, 79
Urger, 108

V

Van Wie's, 60
Vandervoort, Al, 63, 66, 79, 81, 82, 106
Vandervoort, Elmer, 80
Vandervoort, Julia, 79
Vandervoort, Louis, 33, 39, 66, 71, 79, 81 -82, 101, 105 -106, 108
Vandervoort, Will, 82
Victory Mills, 63

W

Wait, Hank, 71
Walrod, Alice Etta, 111

Walrod, Henry, 111
water,
drinking/cooking, 87
Esopus Island, 87
Split Rock, 87
Waterford sidecut, 10
Waterford, NY, 1 -2, 10, 18, 28, 33 -34, 39, 51, 55 -56, 59, 69, 75, 83, 101, 108, 112
Watervliet, NY, 9
Weighlock, 10, 55
Welch, Eddie, 17, 79
Western Canal
(see Erie Canal)
West Troy, NY, 9
West Virginia Pulp and
Paper Co., 59, 80
Wetherbee, 32
Whaley, Jud, 63, 65
Whitehall, NY, 1 -2, 5, 10, 18, 28, 32 -33, 37, 39, 51, 59, 67, 82, 89 -90
Wilbur's Basin, 60, 80, 106
William H. Nealer,107
William P. Dalton,80
Williams Saloon, 65
Willow Grocery Store, 91
Wilmington, De., 5
Wood Creek, 31 -32, 51, 105
Wood Lock, 31, 51, 82
Wood, Eddie, 37